Views from the Real World

Paris, 1922

Gurdjïeff

Views from the Real World

Early Talks
in Moscow, Essentuki, Tiflis, Berlin, London,
Paris, New York and Chicago
As Recollected by His Pupils

A Dutton  *Paperback*

NEW YORK
E. P. DUTTON

Published in the United States by E. P. Dutton,
a division of NAL Penguin Inc.,
2 Park Avenue, New York, N.Y. 10016.

This Dutton Paperback edition first published in 1975 by
E. P. Dutton & Co., Inc.
Copyright © 1973 by Triangle Editions, Inc.
All rights reserved. Printed in the U.S.A.

11 13 15 17 19 20 18 16 14 12

Published simultaneously in Canada
by Fitzhenry & Whiteside Limited, Toronto

ISBN: 0-525-48251-2
Library of Congress Catalog Card Number: 73-10482

Introduction

Gurdjieff is becoming well known as a pioneer of the new current of thought about man's situation, such as has been provided throughout the ages at times of transition in human history.

A quarter century after his death, his name has emerged from a background of rumor and he is recognized today as a great spiritual force, who saw clearly the direction modern civilization is taking and who set to work behind the scenes to prepare people in the West to discover for themselves and eventually to diffuse among mankind the certainty that Being is the only indestructible reality.

The outline of his life is familiar to readers of his Second and Third Series, *Meetings with Remarkable Men* (published in 1963) and *Life Is Real Only Then, When "I Am"* (privately printed in 1975).

Born on the frontier of Russia and Turkey in 1877 "in strange, almost biblical circumstances," his education as a boy left him with many unanswered questions and he set out when quite young in search of men who had achieved a complete knowledge of human life. His early travels to unidentified places in Central Asia and the Middle East lasted twenty years.

On his return, he began to gather pupils in Moscow before the first World War and continued his work with a small party of followers while moving, during the year of the Russian revolution, to Essentuki in the Caucasus, and then through Tiflis, Constantinople, Berlin and London to the Chateau du Prieuré near Paris, where he reopened his Institute for the Harmonious Development of Man in 1922 on a larger scale.

After his first visit to America in 1924, a motor accident interrupted further plans for the Institute. From 1924 to 1935, he turned all his energies to writing.

The rest of his life was spent in intensive work, chiefly with French pupils in Paris where, after completing arrangements for posthumous publication in New York and London of his First Series, *Beelzebub's Tales to His Grandson*, he died in 1949.

What does his teaching consist of? And is it intelligible to everybody?

He showed that the evolution of man—a theme prominent in the scientific thinking of his youth—cannot be approached through mass influences but is the result of individual inner growth; that such an inner opening was the aim of all religions, of all the Ways, but requires a direct and precise knowledge of changes in the quality of each man's inner consciousness: a knowledge which had been preserved in places he had visited, but can only be acquired with an experienced guide through prolonged self-study and "work on oneself."

Through the order of his ideas, and the exercises which he changed repeatedly, the minds of all who came to him were opened to the most complete dissatisfaction with themselves and at the same time to the vast scale of their inner possibilities, in a way that none of them ever forgot.

The statement of his teaching which Gurdjieff presented in *Beelzebub's Tales* has to be searched for within a panorama of the whole history of human culture, from the creation of life on the planet through the rise and fall of civilizations up to modern times.

Fortunately, some record exists of his actual words and his direct instructions given in conversations, talks and lectures at the Prieuré, and as he traveled from one city to the next with his pupils, often in difficult conditions. These are the talks contained in this book.

They consist of notes put together from memory by some of those who heard the talks and recorded them faithfully afterwards. Treasured and carefully protected from misuse, even the fact of the existence of these notes became known only gradually.

Incomplete as they are, even fragmentary in some cases, the collection is an authentic rendering of Gurdjieff's approach to work on oneself, as expressed to his pupils at the required moment. Moreover, even in these notes from memory, it is striking that regardless of the variety of his audiences—on some occasions, people long familiar with his idea, on others people invited to meet him for the first time— there is always the same human tone of voice, the same man evoking an intimate response in each of his listeners.

In her foreword to the first edition of this book, Jeanne de Salzmann, who spent thirty years with Gurdjieff from 1919 in Tiflis until his death, and participated in all the stages of his work, even carrying the responsibility for his groups in the last ten years of his life, states that:

"Today, when Gurdjieff's teaching is being studied and put into practice by sizeable research groups in America, Europe and even Asia, it seems desireable to shed some light on a fundamental characteristic of his teaching, namely, that while the truth sought for was always the same, the forms through which he helped his pupils approach it served only for a limited time. As soon as a new understanding had been reached, the form would change.

"Readings, talks, discussions and studies, which had been the main feature of work for a period of time and had stimulated the intelligence to the point of opening it to an entirely new way of seeing, were for some reason or other suddenly brought to an end.

"This put the pupil on the spot. What his intellect had become capable of conceiving had now to be experienced with his feeling.

"Unexpected conditions were brought about in order to upset habits. The only possibility of facing the new situation was through a deep self-examination, with that total sincerity which alone can change the quality of human feeling.

"Then the body, in its turn, was required to collect all the energy of its attention, to attune itself to an order which it was there to serve.

"After this, the experience could follow its course on another level.

"As Gurdjieff himself used to say: 'All the parts which constitute the human being must be informed—informed in the only way which is appropriate for each of them—otherwise the development will be lopsided and unable to go further.'

"The ideas are a summons, a summons towards another world, a call from one who knows and who is able to show us the way. But the transformation of the human being requires something more. It can only be achieved if there is a real meeting between the conscious force which descends and the total commitment that answers it. This brings about a fusion.

"A new life can then appear in a new set of conditions which only someone with an objective consciousness can create and develop.

"But to understand this one must have passed through all the stages of this development. Without such experience and understanding the work will lose its effectiveness and the conditions will be wrongly interpreted; they will not be brought at the right moment and situations and efforts will remain on the level of ordinary life, uselessly repeating themselves."

Glimpses of Truth is an account of a conversation with Gurdjieff written by a Moscow pupil in 1914 and mentioned by P. D. Ouspensky in *In Search of the Miraculous*. It is the first—and probably the only—example of a series of essays on Gurdjieff's ideas projected by him at that period. The author of it is not known.

The *Talks* have been compared and regrouped with the help of Madame Thomas de Hartmann, who from 1917 in Essentuki was present at all these meetings and could thus guarantee their authenticity.

It will be noticed that passages in several of the talks (including those beginning "For an exact study," "To all my questions" and "The two rivers") are in fact expressions of the material which Gurdjieff used later in only a slightly different form when writing the last chapter of *Beelzebub's Tales to his Grandson*.

Some of the *Aphorisms* have been published before in accounts of life at the Prieuré. They were inscribed in a special alphabet, known only to the pupils, above the walls of the Study House where his talks were given. A painting of one of the Aphorisms in this alphabet has been used as the cover design for this book. It reads in Russian, "Remember yourself always and everywhere."

Views from the Real World

Contents

[xi]

I

Glimpses of Truth

written by one of Gurdjieff's circle in Moscow

Strange events, incomprehensible from the ordinary point of view, have guided my life. I mean those events which influence a man's inner life, radically changing its direction and aim and creating new epochs in it. I call them incomprehensible because their connection was clear only to me. It was as though some invisible person, in pursuit of a definite aim, had placed in the path of my life circumstances which, at the very moment of my need, I found there as if by chance. Guided by such events, I became accustomed from my early years to look with great penetration into the circumstances surrounding me and to try to grasp the principle connecting them, and to find in their interrelations a broader, more complete explanation. I must say that in every exterior result it was the hidden cause evoking it that interested me most.

One day in the course of my life, in this same apparently strange way, I found myself face to face with occultism, and became interested in it as though in a deep and harmonious philosophical system. But at the very moment when I had reached something more than mere interest, I again lost, as suddenly as I had found it, the possibility of proceeding with its systematic study. In other words, I was thrown entirely on

my own resources. This loss seemed a senseless failure, but I
later recognized in it a necessary stage in the course of my life
and one full of deep meaning. This recognition came only
much later, however. I did not deviate but went forward on
my own responsibility and at my own risk. Insuperable obstacles confronted me, forcing me to retreat. Vast horizons
opened to my vision and as I hastened forward I often slipped
or became entangled. Losing, as it seemed, what I had discovered, I remained wandering round on the same spot, as though
fogbound. In searching I made many efforts and did apparently useless work, rewarded inadequately by results. Today, I
see that no effort went unrewarded and that every mistake
served to guide me toward the truth.

I plunged into the study of occult literature, and without exaggeration can say that I not only read but mastered patiently
and perseveringly the greater part of the available material,
trying to grasp the sense and to understand what was hidden
between the lines. All this only served to convince me that I
would never succeed in finding what I sought in books:
though I glimpsed the outlines of a majestic structure, I could
not see it clearly and distinctly.

I searched for those who might have interests in common
with me. Some seemed to have found something, but on closer
examination I saw that they, like myself, were groping in the
dark. I still hoped in the end to find what I needed; I looked
for a living man, able to give me more than I could find in a
book. Perseveringly and obstinately I sought and, after each
failure, hope revived again and led me to a new search. With
this in view I visited Egypt, India and other countries. Among
those encountered were many who left no trace, but some
were of great importance.

Several years passed; among my acquaintances I counted
some to whom, by the community of our interests, I was bound
more durably. One in close touch with me was a certain A.
The two of us had spent not a few sleepless nights, racking our
brains over several passages in a book we did not understand

and searching for appropriate explanations. In this way we had come to know each other intimately.

But during the last six months I had begun to notice, first at rare intervals, and then more frequently, something odd about him. It was not that he had turned his back on me, but he had seemed to grow cooler toward the search, which had not ceased to be vital to me. At the same time I saw he had not forgotten it. He often expressed thoughts and made comments which became fully comprehensible only after long reflection. I remarked on it more than once, but he always skillfully avoided conversations on this subject.

I must confess that this growing indifference of A., who had been the constant companion of my work, led to gloomy reflections. Once I spoke to him openly about it—I scarcely remember in which way.

"Who told you," objected A., "that I am deserting you? Wait a little and you will see clearly that you are mistaken."

But for some reason neither these remarks, nor some others which at the time seemed strange to me, caught my interest. Perhaps because I was occupied in reconciling myself to the idea of my complete isolation.

So it continued. It is only now that I see how, in spite of an apparent capacity for observation and analysis, I overlooked the main factor, continually before my eyes, in a way which was unpardonable. But let the facts speak for themselves.

One day about the middle of November, I spent the evening with a friend of mine. The conversation was on a subject of little interest to me. During a pause in the talk, my host said, "By the way, knowing your partiality for occultism I think an item in today's *Golos Moskvi* [*The Voice of Moscow*] would interest you." And he pointed out an article headed "Round about the Theatre."

It spoke, giving a brief summary, about the scenario of a medieval mystery, *The Struggle of the Magicians:* a ballet written by G. I. Gurdjieff, an orientalist who was well-known in

Moscow. The mention of occultism, the title itself and the contents of the scenario, aroused my great interest, but none of the people present could give any more information about it. My host, a keen amateur of ballet, admitted that in his circle he knew of no one corresponding to the description in the article. I cut it out, with his permission, and took it away with me.

I will not weary you with an exposition of my reasons for being interested in this article. But it was as a consequence of them that I took a firm resolve on Saturday morning to find Mr. Gurdjieff, the writer of the scenario, at all costs.

That same evening when A. called upon me, I showed him the article. I told him that it was my intention to search for Mr. Gurdjieff, and asked his opinion.

A. read the article and, glancing at me, said: "Well, I wish you success. As far as I am concerned, it does not interest me. Haven't we had enough of such tales?" And he put the article aside with an air of indifference. Such an attitude toward this question was so chilling that I gave up and retreated into my thoughts; A. was also thoughtful. Our conversation was halted. There was a long silence, interrupted by A., who put his hand on my shoulder.

"Look here," he said, "don't be offended. I had my own reasons, which I will explain later, for answering you as I did. But first, I shall ask a few questions which are *so* serious"—he emphasized the word "so"—"you cannot know how serious they are." Somewhat astonished by this pronouncement, I answered, "Ask."

"Do, please, tell me why you wish to find this Mr. Gurdjieff? How will you look for him? What aim will you follow? And if your search is successful, in what way will you approach him?"

At first unwillingly, but encouraged by the seriousness of A.'s manner, as well as by questions he occasionally put, I explained the direction of my thinking.

When I had finished, A. went over what I had said and added, "I can tell you that you won't find anything."

"How can that be?" I replied. "It seems to me that the ballet scenario of *The Struggle of the Magicians,* apart from being dedicated to Geltzer, is hardly so unimportant that its author could be lost without a trace."

"It is not a question of the author. You may find him. But he won't talk with you as he *could,*" said A.

I flared up at this: "Why do you imagine that he . . .?" "I do not *imagine* anything," A. interrupted. "I *know.* But not to keep you in suspense I tell you, I know this scenario well, very well. What is more I know its author, Mr. Gurdjieff, personally, and have known him for a long time. The way you have elected to find him might lead you to make his acquaintance, but not in the way that you would wish. Believe me, if you will allow me a piece of friendly advice, wait a little longer. I will try to arrange you a meeting with Mr. Gurdjieff in the way you wish . . . Well, I must be going."

In the greatest astonishment I seized him. "Wait! You can't go yet. How did you come to know him? Who is he? Why have you never told me about him before?"

"Not so many questions," said A. "I categorically refuse to answer them now. In due course I will answer. Set your mind at rest meanwhile; I promise to do everything I can to introduce you."

In spite of my most insistent demands A. refused to reply, adding that it was in my interest not to delay him any longer.

About two o'clock on Sunday, A. telephoned me and said briefly: "If you wish, be at the railroad station at seven o'clock." "And where are we going?" I asked. "To Mr. Gurdjieff," he replied, and hung up.

"He certainly does not stand on ceremony with me," flashed through my mind, "he did not even ask me whether I could go, and I happen to have some important business tonight. Besides, I have no idea how far we have to go. When shall we be back? How shall I explain at home?" But then I decided that A. was not likely to have overlooked the circumstances of my life; so the "important" business quickly lost its importance and I began to await the appointed hour. Being impatient, I arrived at the station almost an hour too early, and waited for A.

Finally he appeared. "Come, quick," he said, hurrying me. "I have the tickets. I was delayed and we are late."

A porter was following us with some big boxes. "What is that?" I asked A. "Are we going away for a year?" "No," he replied laughing. "I'll come back with you; the boxes don't concern us."

We took our seats and, being alone in the compartment, nobody disturbed our conversation.

"Are we going far?" I asked.

A. named one of the country resorts near Moscow and added, "To save you more enquiries I will tell you everything possible; but the greater part will be for you alone. Of course, you are right to be interested in Mr. Gurdjieff as a person, but I will tell you only a few external facts about him, to give you your bearings. As for my personal opinions about him I will keep silent, so that you may take in your own impressions more fully. We shall return to this matter later."

Settling comfortably into his seat, he began to talk.

He told me that Mr. Gurdjieff had spent many years wandering in the East with a definite purpose and had been in places inaccessible to Europeans; that two or three years ago he had come to Russia and had then lived in Petersburg, devoting his efforts and his knowledge mainly to work of his own. Not long ago he had moved to Moscow and had rented a country house near the town, so as to be able to work in retirement undisturbed. In accordance with a rhythm known only to himself he would periodically visit Moscow, returning to his work again after a certain interval. He did not think it necessary, I gathered, to tell his Moscow acquaintances about his country house and he did not receive anyone there.

"As to how I came to know him," said A., "we will talk of that another time. That, too, is far from commonplace."

A. went on to say that very early in his acquaintance with Mr. Gurdjieff he had spoken about me and wished to introduce us; not only had he refused, but he had actually forbidden A. to tell me anything about him. On account of my persistent demand to make Mr. Gurdjieff's acquaintance and my aim of so doing, A. had decided to ask him once more. He had seen him, after leaving me the previous night, and Mr. Gurdjieff, after asking many detailed questions about me, had agreed to see me and himself had proposed that A. should bring me to him that evening, in the country.

"In spite of my knowing you for so many years," said A., "he certainly knows you better than I do, from what I have told him. Now you realize that it was not just imagination when I told you that you could not obtain anything in the ordinary way. Don't forget, a great exception is being made for you and none of those who know him have been where you are going. Even those closest to him do not suspect the existence of his retreat. You owe this exception to my recommendation, so please do not put me in an awkward position."

Several more questions produced no reply from A., but when I asked him about *The Struggle of the Magicians* he told me its contents in some detail. When I questioned him about something which struck me as incongruous, A. told me Mr. Gurdjieff would speak about it himself, if he thought it necessary.

This conversation aroused in me a multitude of thoughts and conjectures. After a silence, I turned to A. with a question. A. gave me a somewhat perplexed glance and, after a short pause, said: "Collect your thoughts, or you will make a fool of yourself. We are nearly there. Don't make me regret having brought you. Remember what you said about your aim yesterday."

After this he said nothing.

At the station we left the train in silence and I offered to carry one of the boxes. It weighed at least seventy pounds, and the box carried by A. was probably no lighter. A four-seated sleigh was waiting for us. Silently we took our places, and drove all the way in the same deep silence. After about fifteen

minutes the sleigh stopped before a gate. A large two-storied
country house was dimly visible at the far end of the garden.
Preceded by our driver carrying the luggage, we entered the
unlocked gate and walked to the house along a path cleared of
snow. The door was ajar. A. rang the bell.

After some time a voice asked, "Who's there?" A. gave his
name. "How are you?" the same voice called through the half-
open door. The driver carried the boxes into the house and
went out again. "Let us go in, now," said A., who appeared to
have been waiting for something.

We passed through a dark hallway into a dimly lit ante-
room. A. closed the door after us; there was nobody in the
room. "Take your things off," he said shortly, pointing to a
peg. We removed our coats.

"Give me your hand; don't be afraid, you won't fall." Clos-
ing the door firmly behind him, A. led me forward into a completely dark room. The floor was covered with a soft carpet on
which our steps made no sound. I put out my free hand in the
dark and felt a heavy curtain, which ran the whole length of
what seemed to be a large room, forming a kind of passage to
a second door. "Keep your aim before you," A. whispered, and
lifting a carpet hung across a door, he pushed me ahead into a
lighted room.

Opposite the door a middle-aged man was sitting against
the wall on a low ottoman, with his feet crossed in Eastern
fashion; he was smoking a curiously shaped water pipe which
stood on a low table in front of him. Beside the pipe stood a
small cup of coffee. These were the first things that caught my
eye.

As we entered, Mr. Gurdjieff—for it was he—raised his hand
and, glancing calmly at us, greeted us with a nod. Then he
asked me to sit down, indicating the ottoman beside him. His
complexion betrayed his Oriental origin. His eyes particularly
attracted my attention, not so much in themselves as by the
way he looked at me when he greeted me, not as if he saw me
the first time but as though he had known me long and well. I

sat down and glanced round the room. Its appearance was so
unusual to a European that I wish to describe it in more detail.
There was no area not covered, either by carpets or hangings
of some sort. A single enormous rug covered the floor of this
spacious room. Even its walls were hung with carpets which
also draped the doors and windows; the ceiling was covered
with ancient silk shawls of resplendent colors, astonishingly
beautiful in their combination. These were drawn together in
a strange pattern toward the center of the ceiling. The light
was concealed behind a dull glass shade of peculiar form re-
sembling a huge lotus flower, which produced a white, dif-
fused glow.

Another lamp, which gave a similar light, stood on a high
stand to the left of the ottoman on which we sat. Against the
left-hand wall was an upright piano covered with antique dra-
peries, which so camouflaged its form that without its candle-
sticks I should not have guessed what it was. On the wall over
the piano, set against a large carpet, hung a collection of
stringed instruments of unusual shapes, among which were
also flutes. Two other collections also adorned the wall. One of
ancient weapons with some slings, yataghans, daggers and
other things, was behind and above our heads. On the opposite wall, suspended by fine white wire, a number of old
carved pipes were arranged in a harmonious group.

Underneath this latter collection, on the floor against the
wall, lay a long row of big cushions covered with a single carpet. In the left-hand corner, at the end of the row, was a
Dutch stove draped with an embroidered cloth. The corner on
the right was decorated with a particularly fine color combination; in it hung an ikon of St. George the Victor, set with precious stones. Beneath it stood a cabinet in which were several
small ivory statues of different sizes; I recognized Christ, Bud-
dha, Moses and Mahomet; the rest I could not see very well.

Another low ottoman stood against the right-hand wall. On
either side of it were two small carved ebony tables and on
one was a coffee-pot with a heating lamp. Several cushions and

hassocks were strewn about the room in careful disorder. All the furniture was adorned with tassels, gold embroidery and gems. As a whole, the room produced a strangely cosy impression which was enhanced by a delicate scent that mingled agreeably with an aroma of tobacco.

Having examined the room, I turned my eyes to Mr. Gurdjieff. He looked at me, and I had the distinct impression that he took me in the palm of his hand and weighed me. I smiled involuntarily, and he looked away from me calmly and without haste. Glancing at A., he said something to him. He did not look at me again in this way and the impression was not repeated.

A. was seated on a big cushion beside the ottoman, in the same posture as Mr. Gurdjieff, which seemed to have become habitual to him. Presently he rose and, taking two large pads of paper and two pencils from a small table, he gave one to Mr. Gurdjieff and kept the other. Indicating the coffee-pot he said to me, "When you want coffee, help yourself. I am going to have some now." Following his example, I poured out a cup and, returning to my place, put it beside the water pipe on the small table.

I then turned to Mr. Gurdjieff and, trying to express myself as briefly and definitely as possible, I explained why I had come. After a short silence, Mr. Gurdjieff said: "Well, let's not lose any precious time," and asked me what I really wanted.

To avoid repetition, I will note certain peculiarities of the conversation that followed. First of all I must mention a rather strange circumstance, one I did not notice at the moment, perhaps because I had not time to think about it. Mr. Gurdjieff spoke Russian neither fluently nor correctly. Sometimes he searched for a considerable time for the words and expressions he needed, and turned constantly to A. for help. He would say two or three words to him; A. seemed to catch his thought in the air, and to develop and complete it, and give it a form intelligible to me. He seemed well acquainted with the subject under discussion. When Mr. Gurdjieff spoke, A. watched him with attention. With a word Mr. Gurdjieff would show him some new meaning, and would swiftly change the direction of A.'s thought.

Of course A.'s knowledge of me very much helped him to enable me to understand Mr. Gurdjieff. Many times with a single hint A. would evoke a whole category of thoughts. He served as a sort of transmitter between Mr. Gurdjieff and myself. At first Mr. Gurdjieff had to appeal to A. constantly, but as the subject broadened and developed, embracing new areas, Mr. Gurdjieff turned to A. less and less often. His speech flowed more freely and naturally; the necessary words seemed to come of themselves, and I could have sworn that, by the end of the conversation, he was speaking the clearest unaccented Russian, his words succeeding one another fluently and calmly; they were rich in color, similes, vivid examples, broad and harmonious perspectives.

In addition, both of them illustrated the conversation with various diagrams and series of numbers, which, taken together, formed a graceful system of symbols—a sort of script—in which one number could express a whole group of ideas. They quoted numerous examples from physics and mechanics, and especially brought material from chemistry and mathematics.

Mr. Gurdjieff sometimes turned to A. with a short remark which referred to something A. was familiar with, and occasionally mentioned names. A. indicated by a nod that he understood, and the conversation proceeded without interruption. I also realized that, while teaching me, A. was learning himself.

Another peculiarity was that I had to ask very rarely. As soon as a question arose and before it could be formulated, the development of the thought had already given the answer. It was as though Mr. Gurdjieff had known in advance and anticipated the questions which might arise. Once or twice I made a false move by asking about some matter that I had not troubled to get clear myself. But I will speak about this at the right place.

I can best compare the direction of the current of the conversation to a spiral. Mr. Gurdjieff, having taken some main idea, and after having broadened it and given it depth, completed the cycle of his reasoning by a return to the starting point, which I saw, as it were, below me, more broadly and in greater detail. A new cycle, and again there was a clearer and more precise idea of the breadth of the original thought.

I do not know how I should have felt, had I been forced to speak with Mr. Gurdjieff *tête-à-tête*. The presence of A., his calm and serious enquiring attitude toward the conversation, must have impressed itself upon me without my knowing it.

Taken as a whole, what was said brought me an inexpressible pleasure I had never before experienced. The outlines of that majestic edifice which had been dark and incomprehensible to me, were now clearly delineated, and not only the outlines but some of the façade's details.

I should like to describe, even if it is only approximately, the essence of this conversation. Who knows but that it may not help someone in a position similar to my own? This is the purpose of my sketch.

"You are acquainted with occult literature," began Mr. Gurdjieff, "and so I will refer to the formula you know from the *Emerald Tablets*: 'As above, so below.' It is easy to start to build the foundation of our discussion from this. At the same time I must say that there is no need to use occultism as the base from which to approach the understanding of truth. Truth speaks for itself in whatever form it is manifested. You will understand this fully only in the course of time, but I wish to give you today at least a grain of understanding. So, I repeat, I begin with the occult formula because I am speaking to *you*. I know you have tried to decipher this formula. I know that you 'understand' it. But the understanding you have now is only a dim and distant reflection of the divine brilliance.

"It is not about the formula itself that I shall speak to you—I am not going to analyze or decipher it. Our conversation will

not be about the literal meaning; we shall take it only as a
starting point for our discussion. And to give you an idea of
our subject, I may say that I wish to speak about the overall
unity of all that exists—about unity in multiplicity. I wish to
show you two or three facets of a precious crystal, and to draw
your attention to the pale images faintly reflected in them.

"I know you understand about the unity of the laws govern-
ing the universe, but this understanding is speculative—or
rather, theoretical. It is not enough to understand with the
mind, it is necessary to feel with your being the absolute
truth and immutability of this fact; only then will you be able,
consciously and with conviction, to say 'I know.'"

Such was the sense of the words with which Mr. Gurdjieff
began the conversation. He then proceeded to describe vividly
the sphere in which the life of all mankind moves, with a
thought which illustrated the Hermetic formula he had
quoted. By analogies he passed from the little ordinary happenings in the life of an individual to the great cycles in the
life of the whole of mankind. By means of such parallels he un-
derscored the cyclic action of the law of analogy within the di-
minutive sphere of terrestrial life. Then, in the same way, he
passed from mankind to what I would call the life of the earth,
representing it as an enormous organism like that of man, and
in terms of physics, mechanics, biology and so on. I watched
the illumination of his thought come increasingly into focus
on one point. The inevitable conclusion of all that he said was
the great law of tri-unity: the law of the three principles of action, resistance and equipoise: the active, passive and neutral
principles. Now resting upon the solid foundation of the earth,
and armed with this law, he applied it, with a bold flight of
thought, to the whole solar system. Now his thought no longer
moved toward this law of tri-unity, but already out from it,
emphasizing it more and more, and manifesting it in the step
nearest to man, that of Earth and Sun. Then, with a brief
phrase, he passed beyond the limits of the solar system. Astronomical data first flashed forth, then appeared to dwindle and

disappear before the infinity of space. There remained only one great thought, issuing from the same great law. His words sounded slow and solemn, and at the very same moment seemed to diminish and lose their significance. Behind them could be sensed the pulse of a tremendous thought.

"We have come to the brink of the abyss which can never be bridged by ordinary human reason. Do you feel how superfluous and useless words have become? Do you feel how powerless reason by itself is here? We have approached the principle behind all principles." Having said this, he became silent, his gaze thoughtful.

Spellbound by the beauty and grandeur of this thought, I had gradually ceased to listen to the words. I could say that I felt them, that I grasped his thought not with my reason but by intuition. Man far below was reduced to nothingness, and disappeared leaving no trace. I was filled with a sense of closeness to the Great Inscrutable, and with the deep consciousness of my personal nothingness.

As though divining my thoughts, Mr. Gurdjieff asked: "We started with man, and where is he? But great, all-embracing is the law of unity. Everything in the Universe is one, the difference is only of scale; in the infinitely small we shall find the same laws as in the infinitely great. As above, so below.

"The sun has risen over the mountaintops above; the valley is still in darkness. So reason, transcending the human condition, regards the divine light, while for those dwelling below all is darkness. Again I repeat, all in the world is one; and since reason is also one, human reason forms a powerful instrument for investigation.

"Now, having come to the beginning, let us descend to the earth from which we came, we shall find its place in the order of the structure of the Universe. Look!"

He made a single sketch and, with a passing reference to the laws of mechanics, delineated the scheme of the construction of the Universe. With numbers and figures in harmonious, systematic columns, multiplicity within unity began to appear.

The figures began to be clothed with meaning, the ideas which had been dead began to come to life. One and the same law ruled all; with delighted understanding I pursued the harmonious development of the Universe. His scheme took its rise from a Great Beginning and ended with the earth.

While he made this exposition, Mr. Gurdjieff noted the necessity of what he called a "shock" reaching a given place from outside and connecting the two opposite principles into one balanced unity. This corresponded to the point of application of force in a balanced system of forces in mechanics.

"We have reached the point to which our terrestrial life is linked," Mr. Gurdjieff said, "and for the present will not go further. In order to examine more closely what has just been said, and to emphasize once more the unity of the laws, we will take a simple scale and apply it, increased proportionately to the measurement of the microcosmos." And he asked me to choose something familiar of regular structure, such as the spectrum of white light, musical scale, and so on. After having thought, I chose the musical scale.

"You have made a good choice," said Mr. Gurdjieff. "As a matter of fact the musical scale, in the form in which it now exists, was constructed in ancient times by those possessed of great knowledge, and you will realize how much it can contribute to the understanding of the principal laws."

He said a few words about the laws of the scale's structure, and particularly stressed the gaps, as he called them, which exist in every octave between the notes mi and fa and also between si of one octave and do of the next. Between these notes there are missing half-tones, in both the ascending and descending scales. While in the ascending development of the octave, the notes do, re, fa, sol and la can pass into the next higher tones, the notes mi and si are deprived of this possibility. He explained how these two gaps, according to certain laws depending on the law of tri-unity, were filled in by new octaves of other orders, these octaves within the gaps playing a part similar to that of the half-tones in the evolutionary or involutionary process of the octave. The principal octave was similar to a tree trunk, sending out branches of subordinate octaves. The seven principal notes of the octave and the two gaps, "bearers of new directions," gave a total of nine links of a chain, or three groups of three links each.

After this he turned to the structural scheme of the Universe, and from it singled out that "ray" whose course led through the earth.

The original powerful octave, whose notes of apparently ever-lessening force included the sun, the earth and the moon, had inevitably fallen, according to the law of tri-unity, into three subordinate octaves. Here the role of the gaps in the octave and the differences in their nature were defined and made clear to me. Of the two intervals, mi-fa and si-do, one was more active—more of the nature of will—while the other played the passive part. The "shocks" of the original scheme, which was not altogether clear to me, were also the rule here, and appeared in a new light.

In the division of this "ray," the place, the role and the destiny of mankind became clear. Moreover the possibilities of the individual man were more apparent.

"It may seem to you," said Mr. Gurdjieff, "that in following the aim of unity, we have deviated from it somewhat in the direction of learning about multiplicity. What I am going to explain now you will no doubt understand. At the same time I am certain that this understanding will chiefly refer to the structural part of what is set forth. Try to fix your interest and attention not on its beauty, its harmony and its ingenuity—and even this side you will not understand entirely—but on the spirit, on what lies hidden behind the words, on the inner content. Otherwise you will see only form, deprived of life. Now, you will see one of the facets of the crystal and, if your eye could perceive the reflection in it, you would draw nearer to the truth itself."

Then Mr. Gurdjieff began to explain the way in which fundamental octaves are combined with secondary octaves subor-

dinate to them; how these, in their turn, send forth new octaves of the next order, and so on. I could compare it to the
process of growth or, more aptly, to the formation of a tree.
Out of a straight vigorous trunk boughs branch out, producing
in their turn small branches and twigs, and then leaves appear
on them. One could already sense the process of formation of
veins.

I must admit that, in fact, my attention was chiefly attracted
to the harmony and beauty of the system. In addition to the
octaves growing, like branches from a trunk, Mr. Gurdjieff
pointed out that each note of every octave appears, from another point of view, as a whole octave: the same was true
everywhere. These "inner" octaves I should compare to the
concentric layers of a tree trunk which fit one within the
other.

All these explanations were given in very general terms.
They emphasized the lawful character of the structure. But for
the examples which accompanied it, it might have been found
rather theoretical. The examples gave it life, and sometimes it
seemed that I really began to guess what was hidden behind
the words. I saw that in this consistency in the structure of the
universe, all the possibilities, all the combinations without exception, had been foreseen; the infinity of infinities was fore-
shadowed. And yet, at the same time, I could not see it, because my reason faltered before the immensity of the concept.
Again I was filled with a dual sensation—the nearness of the
possibility of all-knowing and the consciousness of its inacces-
sibility.

Once more I heard Mr. Gurdjieff's words echoing my feelings: "No ordinary reason is enough to enable a man to take
the Great Knowledge to himself, and make it his inalienable
possession. Nevertheless it *is* possible for him. But first he must
shake the dust from his feet. Vast efforts, tremendous labors,
are needed to come into possession of the wings on which it is
possible to rise. It is many times easier to drift with the current, to pass with it from one octave to another; but that takes

immeasurably longer than, alone, to wish and to do. The way is hard, the ascent becomes increasingly steeper as it goes on, but one's strength also increases. A man becomes tempered and with each ascending step his view grows wider. Yes, there *is* the possibility."

I saw indeed that this possibility existed. Although not yet knowing what it was, I saw that it was there. I find it hard to put into words what became more and more understandable. I saw that the reign of law, now becoming apparent to me, was really all-inclusive; that what appeared at first sight to be a violation of a law, on closer examination only confirmed it. One could say without exaggeration that while "exceptions prove the rule," at the same time they were not exceptions. For those who can understand I would say that, in Pythagorean terms, I recognized and felt how Will and Fate—spheres of action of Providence—coexist, while mutually competing; how, without blending or separating, they intermingle. I do not nurture any hope that such contradictory words can convey or make clear what I understand; at the same time I can find nothing that is better.

"You see," Mr. Gurdjieff went on, "that he who possesses a full and complete understanding of the system of octaves, as it might be called, possesses the key to the understanding of Unity, since he understands all that is seen—all happenings, all things in their essence—for he knows their place, cause and effect.

"At the same time you see clearly that this consists of a more detailed development of the original scheme, a more precise representation of the law of unity, and that all we have said and are going to say is nothing but a development of the principal idea of unity. That a full, distinct, clear consciousness of this law is precisely the Great Knowledge to which I referred.

"Speculations, suppositions and hypotheses do not exist for him who possesses such a knowledge. Expressed more definitely, he knows everything by 'measure, number and weight.'

Everything in the Universe is material: *therefore the Great Knowledge is more materialistic than materialism.*

"A look at chemistry will make this more intelligible." He demonstrated how chemistry, in studying matter of various densities without a knowledge of the law of octaves, contains an error which affects the end results. Knowing this, and making certain corrections, based on the law of octaves, brings these results into full accord with those reached by calculation. In addition he pointed out that the idea of simple substances and elements in contemporary chemistry cannot be accepted from the point of view of the chemistry of octaves, which is "objective chemistry." Matter is the same everywhere; its various qualities depend only on the place it occupies in a certain octave, and on the order of the octave itself.

From this point of view, the hypothetical notion of the atom as an indivisible part of a simple substance or element cannot serve as a model. An atom of a given density, a really existing individuum, must be taken as the smallest quantity of the substance examined which retains all those qualities—chemical, physical and cosmic—which characterize it as a certain note of a definite octave. For instance, in contemporary chemistry there is no atom of water, as water is not a simple substance but a chemical compound of hydrogen and oxygen. Yet from the point of view of "objective chemistry" an "atom" of water is an ultimate and definitive volume of it, even visible to the naked eye. Mr. Gurdjieff added: "Certainly you have to accept this on trust for the present. But those who seek for the Great Knowledge under the guidance of one already in possession of it, must personally work to prove, and verify by investigation, what these atoms of matter of different densities are."

I saw it all in mathematical terms. I became clearly convinced that everything in the Universe is material and that everything can be measured numerically in accordance with the law of octaves. The essential material descends in a series of separate notes of various densities. These were expressed in numbers combined according to certain laws, and that which had seemed immeasurable was measured. What had been referred to as cosmic qualities of matter was made clear. To my great surprise, the atomic weights of certain chemical elements were given as examples, with an explanation showing the error of contemporary chemistry.

In addition, the law of the construction of "atoms" in matter of various densities was shown. As this presentation progressed we passed, almost without my being aware of it, to what might be called "the Earth octave" and so arrived at the place from which we had started—on earth.

"In all that I have told you," Mr. Gurdjieff continued, "my aim was not to communicate any new knowledge. On the contrary I only wished to demonstrate that the knowledge of certain laws makes it possible for a man, without moving from where he is, to count, weigh and measure all that exists—both the infinitely great and the infinitely small. I repeat: everything in the universe is material. Ponder those words and you will understand, at least to some degree, why I used the expression *more materialistic than materialism.* . . . Now we have become acquainted with the laws ruling the life of the Microcosmos and have returned to earth. Remember once more 'As above, so below.'

"I think even now and without further explanation you would not dispute the fact that the life of individual man—the Microcosmos—is ruled by this same law. But let us demonstrate this further, by taking a single example in which certain details will become clearer. Let us take a particular question, the plan of work of the human organism, and examine it."

Mr. Gurdjieff next drew a scheme of the human body and compared it to a three-storied factory, the stories being represented by the head, chest and abdomen. Taken together the factory forms a complete whole. This is an octave of the first order, similar to that with which the examination of the Macrocosmos began. Each of the stories also represents an entire octave of the second order, subordinate to the first. Thus we have three subordinate octaves which are again similar to those in the scheme of the construction of the universe. Each of the three stories receives "food" of a suitable nature from outside, assimilates it and combines it with the materials which have already been processed, and in this way the factory functions to produce a certain kind of material.

"I must point out," Mr. Gurdjieff said, "that, although the design of the factory is good and suitable for production of this material, because of the ignorance of its top administration, it manages the business very uneconomically. What would be the situation of an undertaking if, with a vast and continuous consumption of material, the greater part of the production were to go merely to the maintenance of the factory and the consumption and processing of the material? The remainder of the production is spent uselessly and its purpose unknown. It is necessary to organize the business in accordance with exact knowledge; and it will then bring in a large net income which may be spent at one's discretion. Let us, however, come back to our scheme" . . . and he explained that while the food of the lower story was man's meat and drink, air was the food of the middle story, and that of the upper story was what could be called "impressions."

All these three kinds of food, representing matter of certain densities and qualities, belong to octaves of different orders.

I could not refrain from asking here, "What about thought?" "Thought is material as well as everything else," answered Mr. Gurdjieff. "Methods exist by means of which one can prove not only this but that thought, like all other things, can be weighed and measured. Its density can be determined, and thus the thoughts of an individual may be compared with those of the same man on other occasions. One can define all the qualities of thought. I have already told you that everything in the Universe is material."

After that he showed how these three kinds of food, received in different parts of the human organism, enter at the starting points of the corresponding octaves, interconnected by a certain process of law; each of them therefore represents do of the octave of its own order. The laws of the development of octaves are the same everywhere.

For instance, do of the food octave coming into the stomach, the third do, passes through the corresponding half-tone into re, and by way of the next passage through a half-tone is further converted into mi. Mi, lacking this half-tone, cannot, by way of a natural development, pass independently into fa. It is assisted by the air octave, which enters the chest. As already shown, this is an octave of a higher order, and its do (the second do), having the necessary half-tone for the transition into re, appears to connect up with the mi of the former octave and transmute into fa. That is, it plays the part of the missing half-tone and serves as a shock for the further development of the former octave.

"We will not stop now," said Mr. Gurdjieff, "to examine the octave beginning with the second do, nor that of the first do, which enters at a definite place. This would only complicate the present situation. We have now made sure of the possibility of a further development of the octave under discussion, thanks to the presence of the half-tone. Fa passes through a half-tone into sol and in fact the material received here appears to be the salt of the human organism [the Russian word for salt is *sol.*] This is the highest that can be produced by it." Reverting to numbers, he again made his thought clear in terms of their combinations.

"The further development of the octave transfers sol through a half-tone into la, and the latter through a half-tone into si. Here the octave again stops. A new 'shock' is required for the passage of si into the do of a new octave of the human organism.

"With what I have now said," Mr. Gurdjieff went on, "and our conversation about chemistry, you will be able to draw some valuable conclusions."

At this point, without waiting to clarify a thought which

came into my head, I asked something about the usefulness of
fasting.

Mr. Gurdjieff stopped speaking. A. gave me a reproachful
look and I immediately realized clearly how inappropriate my
question was. I wished to correct my mistake, but had not time
to do so, before Mr. Gurdjieff said: "I wish to show you one experiment, which will make it clear to you," but after exchang-
ing glances with A. and asking him something, he said: "No,
better later," and after a short silence continued: "I see that
your attention is tired, but I am already almost at the end of
what I wanted to tell you today. I had intended to touch in a
very general way upon the course of the development of man,
but it is not so important now. Let us postpone conversation
about that until a more favorable occasion."

"May I conclude from what you say," I asked, "that you will
sometimes permit me to see you, and converse on the questions which interest me?"

"Now that we have begun these conversations," he said, "I
have no objection to continuing them. Much depends on you.
What I mean by this, A. will explain to you in detail." Then,
noticing that I was going to turn to A. for the explanation,
"But not now, some other time," he added. "Now I want to tell
you this. As everything in the Universe is one, so, consequently, everything has equal rights, therefore from this point
of view knowledge can be acquired by a suitable and complete
study, no matter what the starting point is. Only one must
know how to 'learn.' What is nearest to us is man; and you
are the nearest of all men to yourself. Begin with the study of
yourself; remember the saying 'Know thyself.' It is possible
that now it will acquire a more intelligible meaning for you.
To begin with, A. will help you in the measure of his own
force and yours. I advise you to remember well the scheme of
the human organism which I gave you. We shall sometimes return to it in the future, adding to its depth every time. Now A.
and I will leave you alone for a short time, as we have a small

matter to attend to. I recommend that you not puzzle your brains over what we have spoken about, but give them a short rest. Even if you happen to forget something, A. will remind you of it afterwards. Of course it would be better if you did not need to be reminded. Accustom yourself to forget nothing.

"Now, have a cup of coffee; it will do you good."

When they had gone I followed Mr. Gurdjieff's advice, and, pouring out coffee, remained sitting. I realized that Mr. Gurdjieff had concluded from the question about fasting that my attention was tired. And I recognized that my thinking had become feebler and more restricted by the end of the conversation. Therefore, in spite of my strong desire to look through all the diagrams and numbers once more, I decided to give my head a rest, to use Mr. Gurdjieff's expression, and sat with closed eyes trying not to think of anything. But the thoughts arose in spite of my will, and I attempted to drive them out.

In about twenty minutes, A. entered without my hearing him and asked, "Well, how are you?" I had no time to answer him when the voice of Mr. Gurdjieff was heard quite close by, saying to someone, "Do as I have told you and you will see where the mistake is."

Then, lifting the carpet which hung over the door, he came in. Taking the same place and attitude as before, he turned toward me. "I hope you have rested—if only a little. Let us talk now of casual matters, without any definite plan."

I told him that I wanted to ask two or three questions that had no immediate reference to the subject of our conversation but might make clearer the nature of what he had said.

"You and A. have quoted so much from the data of contemporary science that the question spontaneously arises, 'Is the knowledge you speak of accessible to an ignorant, uneducated man?' "

"The material you refer to was quoted only because I spoke to you. You understand, because you have a certain amount of

knowledge of these matters. They helped you to understand
something better. They were only given as examples. This refers to the form of the conversation but not to its essence.
Forms may be very different. I will not say anything now
about the role and significance of contemporary science. This
question could be the subject of a separate conversation. I will
only say this—that the best educated scholar could prove an
absolute ignoramus compared with an illiterate shepherd who
possesses knowledge. This sounds paradoxical, but the understanding of the essence, over which the former spends long
years of minute investigation, will be gained by the latter in an
incomparably fuller degree during one day's meditation. It is a
question of the way of thinking, of the 'density of the thought.'
This term does not convey anything to you at present but in
time it will become clear by itself. What else do you want to
ask?"

"Why is this knowledge so carefully concealed?"

"What leads you to ask this question?"

"Certain things which I had the opportunity of learning in
the course of my acquaintance with occult literature," I answered.

"As far as I can judge," said Mr. Gurdjieff, "you are refer-
ring to the question of so-called 'initiation.' Yes, or no?" I replied in the affirmative, and Mr. Gurdjieff went on: "Yes. The
fact of the matter is that in occult literature much that has
been said is superfluous and untrue. You had better forget all
this. All your researches in this area were a good exercise for
your mind: therein lies their great value, but only there. They
have not given you knowledge, as you yourself confessed.
Judge everything from the point of view of your common
sense. Become the possessor of your own sound ideas, and
don't accept anything on faith; and when you, yourself, by
way of sound reasoning and argument, come to an unshakable
persuasion, to a full understanding of something, you will have
achieved a certain degree of initiation. Think it over more
deeply. . . . For instance, today I had a conversation with you.

Remember this conversation. Think, and you will agree with me that in essence I have told you nothing new. You knew it all before. The only thing I did was to bring order into your knowledge. I systematized it, but you had it before you saw me. You owe it to the efforts you had already made in this field. It was easy for me to speak to you, thanks to him"—and he pointed to A.—"because he had learned to understand me, and because he knew you. From his account, I knew you and your knowledge, as well as how it was obtained, before you came to me. But in spite of all these favorable conditions, I may confidently say that you have not mastered even a hundredth part of what I said. However, I have given you a clue pointing to the possibility of a new point of view, from which you can illuminate and bring together your former knowledge. And thanks to this work, to your own work, you will be able to reach a much deeper understanding of what I have said. You will 'initiate' yourself.

"In a year's time we may say the same things, but you will not wait during this year in the hope that roast pigeons will fly into your mouth. You will work, and your understanding will change—you will be more 'initiated.' It is impossible to give a man anything that could become his inalienable property without work on his part. Such an initiation cannot exist, but unfortunately people often think so. There is only 'self-initiation.' One can show and direct, but not 'initiate.' The things which you came across in occult literature with regard to this question had been written by people who had lost the key to what they transmitted on, without any verification, from the words of others.

"Every medal has its reverse. The study of occultism offers much, as training for the mind, but often, unfortunately very often, people infected with the poison of mystery, and aiming at practical results, but not possessing a full knowledge of what must be done or how, do themselves irreparable harm. Harmony is violated. It is a hundred times better not to do anything than to act without knowledge. You said that knowledge is concealed. That is not so. It is not concealed, but people are incapable of understanding it. If you begin a conversation about higher mathematical ideas with a man who did not know mathematics, what good would it be? He simply would not understand you. And here the matter is more complicated. I personally should be very glad if I could speak now to somebody, without trying to adapt myself to his understanding, on those subjects which are of interest to me. But if I began to speak to *you* in this way, for instance, you would take me for a madman or worse.

"People have too few words with which to express certain ideas. But *there*, where words do not matter, but their source and the meaning behind them, it should be possible to speak simply. In the absence of understanding it is impossible. You had the opportunity of proving this to yourself today. I should not speak to another person in the same way that I spoke to you, because he would not understand me. You have initiated yourself already to a certain degree. And before speaking one must know and see how much the man understands. Understanding comes only with work.

"So what you call 'concealment' is in fact the impossibility of giving, otherwise everything would be quite different. If, in spite of this, those who know begin to speak, it is useless and quite unproductive. They speak only when they know that the listener understands."

"So then, if, for instance, I wanted to tell somebody what I have learned from you today, would you object?"

"You see," replied Mr. Gurdjieff, "from the very beginning of our conversation, I foresaw the possibility of continuing it. Therefore I told you things which I would not tell you were the contrary the case. I said them in advance, knowing that you are not prepared for them now, but with the intention of giving a certain direction to your reflections on these questions. On closer consideration you will be convinced that it is really so. You will understand precisely what I am speaking about. If you reach this conclusion it will only be to the advantage of the person with whom you speak; you may say as much as you like. Then you will be convinced that something intelligible and clear to you is unintelligible to those who hear. From this point of view such conversations will be useful."

"And what is your attitude toward enlarging the circle with whom relations might begin, by giving them some indication that could help in their work?" I asked.

"I have too little free time to be able to sacrifice it without being certain that it will be of use. Time is of value to me, and I need it for my work; therefore I cannot and do not wish to spend it unproductively. But I have already told you about that."

"No, it was not with the idea of your making new acquaintances that I asked, but in the sense that indications might be given through the press. I think it would take less time than personal conversations."

"In other words you wish to know whether the ideas could be set forth gradually, in a series of outlines, perhaps?"

"Yes," I replied, "but I certainly do not think it would be possible to clarify everything, though it seems to me that it might be possible to indicate a direction leading nearer to the goal."

"You have raised a very interesting question," said Mr. Gurdjieff. "I have often discussed it with some of those with whom I speak. It is not worthwhile repeating now the considerations which were expressed by them and by me. I can only say that we decided in the affirmative, as long ago as last summer. I did not refuse to take part in this experiment, but we were prevented from making it on account of the war."

During the short conversation which followed on this subject, the idea came into my head that if Mr. Gurdjieff did not object to making known to the public at large certain views and methods, it was also possible that the ballet *The Struggle of the Magicians* might contain a hidden meaning, representing not only a work of imagination but a mystery. I asked him a question about it in this sense, mentioning that A. had told me the contents of the scenario.

"My ballet is not a mystery," replied Mr. Gurdjieff. "The purpose of it is to present an interesting and beautiful spectacle. Of course, under the visible forms a certain sense is hidden, but I did not aim at demonstrating or emphasizing it. The chief position in this ballet is occupied by certain dances. I will explain this to you briefly. Imagine that in studying the laws of movement of the celestial bodies, let us say the planets of the solar system, you have constructed a special mechanism for the representation and recording of these laws. In this mechanism every planet is represented by a sphere of appropriate size and is placed at a strictly determined distance from the central sphere, which stands for the sun. You set the mechanism in motion, and all the spheres begin to turn and move in definite paths, reproducing in a lifelike way the laws which govern their movements. This mechanism reminds you of your knowledge.

"In the same way, in the rhythm of certain dances, in the precise movements and combinations of the dancers, certain laws are vividly recalled. Such dances are called sacred. During my journeys in the East, I often saw dances of this kind executed during the performance of sacred rites in some of the ancient temples. These ceremonies are inaccessible, and unknown to Europeans. Some of these dances are reproduced in *The Struggle of the Magicians*. Further, I may tell you that at the basis of *The Struggle of the Magicians* lie three thoughts; but, as I have no hope that they will be understood by the public if I present the ballet alone, I call it simply a spectacle." Mr. Gurdjieff spoke a little more about the ballet and the dances and then went on:

"Such is the origin of the dances, their significance, in the distant past. I will ask you now, has anything in this branch of contemporary art been preserved that could recall, however remotely, its former great meaning and aim? What is to be found here but triviality?" After a short silence, as though waiting for my reply, and gazing sadly and thoughtfully before him, he continued, "Contemporary art as a whole has nothing in common with the ancient sacred art. . . . Perhaps you have thought about it? What is your opinion?"

I explained to him that the question of art, which amongst others interested me, occupied an important place. To be precise, I was interested not so much in the works, that is, in the results of art, but in its role and significance in the life of humanity. I had often discussed this question with those who seemed to be more versed in these matters than I—musicians, painters, and sculptors, artists and men of letters, and also with those simply interested in studying art. I happened to hear a great deal of opinion of many kinds, often contradictory. Some, it is true they were few, called art an amusement of those who lacked occupation; but the majority agreed that art is sacred and that its creation bears in itself the seal of divine inspiration. I had formed no opinion which I could call my firm conviction, and this question had remained open until now. I expressed all this to Mr. Gurdjieff as clearly as possible; he listened to my explanation with attention, and said:

"You are right in saying that there are many contradictory opinions on this subject. Does not that alone prove that people do not know the truth? Where truth is, there cannot be many different opinions. In antiquity that which is now called art served the aim of objective knowledge. And as we said a moment ago, speaking of dances, works of art represented an exposition and a record of the eternal laws of the structure of the universe. Those who devoted themselves to research and thus acquired a knowledge of important laws, embodied them in works of art, just as is done in books today."

At this point Mr. Gurdjieff mentioned some names which were mostly unknown to me and which I have forgotten. Then he went on: "This art did not pursue the aim either of 'beauty' or of producing a likeness of something or somebody. For instance, an ancient statue created by such an artist is neither a

copy of the form of a person nor the expression of a subjective
sensation; it is either the expression of the laws of knowledge,
in terms of the human body, or a means of objective transmission of a state of mind. The form and action, indeed the whole
expression, is according to law."

After a short silence, in which he appeared to be pondering
something, Mr. Gurdjieff went on: "As we have touched upon
art, I will tell you of an episode which happened recently
which will clarify some points in our conversation.

"Among my acquaintances here in Moscow there is a companion of my early childhood, a famous sculptor. When visit-
ing him I noticed in his library a number of books on Hindu
philosophy and occultism. In the course of conversation I
found that he was seriously interested in these matters. Seeing
how helpless he was in making any independent examination
of these related questions, and not wishing to show my own
acquaintance with them, I asked a man who had often talked
with me on these subjects, a certain P., to interest himself in
this sculptor. One day P. told me that the sculptor's interest in
these questions was clearly speculative, that his essence was
not touched by them and that he saw little use in these discussions. I advised him to turn the conversation toward some subject of closer concern to the sculptor. In the course of what
seemed a purely casual talk at which I was present, P. directed
the conversation to the question of art and creation, where-
upon the sculptor explained that he 'felt' the rightness of
sculptural forms and asked, 'Do you know why the statue of
the poet Gogol in the Arbat Place has an excessively long
nose?' And he related how, on looking at this statue sideways,
he felt that 'the soft flow of the profile,' as he put it, was violated at the top of the nose."

"Wishing to test the correctness of this feeling, he decided
to search for Gogol's death mask, which he found, after a long
search, in private hands. He studied the mask, and paid special
attention to the nose. This examination revealed that probably,
when the mask was taken, a small bubble was formed just

where the soft flow of the profile seemed to be violated. The mask maker had filled in the bubble with an unskilled hand, changing the form of the writer's nose. Thus the designer of the monument, not doubting the correctness of the mask, had furnished Gogol with a nose that was not his.

"What can be said of this incident? Is it not evident that such a thing could only happen in the absence of real knowledge?

"While one man uses the mask, fully believing in its correctness, the other, 'feeling' the incorrectness of its execution, looks for a confirmation of his suspicions. Neither is better off than the other.

"But with a knowledge of the laws of proportion in the human body, not only could the end of Gogol's nose have been reconstructed from the mask but the whole of his body could have been built up exactly as it had been from the nose alone. Let us go into this in more detail to make clear exactly what I want to express.

"Today I briefly examined the law of the octave. You saw that with knowledge of this law the place of everything is known and, vice versa, if the place is known, one knows what exists there and its quality. Everything can be calculated; only one must know how to calculate the passage from one octave to another. The human body, like everything that is a whole, bears in itself this regularity of measurement. In accordance with the number of notes of the octave and with the intervals, the human body has nine principal measurements expressed in definite numbers. For individual persons these numbers vary very much—of course within certain limits. The nine principal measurements, giving an entire octave of the first order, are transmuted into the subordinate octaves which, by a wide extension of this subordinate system, give all the measurements of any part of the human body. Every note of an octave is itself a whole octave. Consequently it is necessary to know the rules of correlation and combination, and of transition from one scale to another. Everything is combined by an indissoluble, unchangeable regularity of law. It is as though, around every point, nine more subordinate points were grouped; and so on to the atoms of the atom.

"Knowing the laws of descent, man also knows the laws of ascent, and consequently not only can pass from principal octaves to subordinate ones, but also vice versa. Not only can the nose be reconstructed from the face alone, but also from the nose the entire face and body of a man can be reconstructed inexorably and exactly. There is no search for beauty or resemblance. A creation can be nothing other than what it is. . . .

"This is more exact than mathematics, because here you do not meet with probabilities, and it is achieved not by study of mathematics but by a study of a far deeper and broader kind. *It is understanding which is needed.* In a conversation without understanding, it is possible to talk for decades on the simplest questions without coming to any result.

"A simple question can reveal that a man has not the required attitude of thought, and even with the desire to elucidate the question, the lack of preparation and understanding in the hearer nullifies the words of the speaker. Such 'literal understanding' is very common.

"This episode yet again confirmed what I had long since known and had proved a thousand times. Recently in Petersburg I spoke with a well-known composer. From this conversation I clearly saw how poor his knowledge in the domain of true music was, and how deep the abyss of his ignorance. Remember Orpheus, who taught knowledge by means of music, and you will understand what I call true or sacred music."

Mr. Gurdjieff went on, "For such music special conditions will be needed, and then *The Struggle of the Magicians* would not be a mere spectacle. As it is now there will only be fragments of the music I heard in certain temples, and even such true music would convey nothing to the hearers because the keys to it are lost and perhaps have never been known in the West. The keys to all the ancient arts are lost, were lost many centuries ago. And therefore there is no longer a sacred art embodying laws of the Great Knowledge, and so serving to influence the instincts of the multitude.

"There are no creators today. The contemporary priests of art do not create but imitate. They run after beauty and likeness or what is called originality, without possessing even the necessary knowledge. Not knowing, and not being able to do anything, since they are groping in the dark, they are praised by the crowd, which places them on a pedestal. Sacred art vanished and left behind only the halo which surrounded its servants. All the current words about the divine spark, talent, genius, creation, sacred art, have no solid basis—they are anachronisms. What are these talents? We will talk about them on some suitable occasion.

"Either the shoemaker's craft must be called art, or all contemporary art must be called craft. In what way is a shoemaker sewing fashionable custom shoes of beautiful design inferior to an artist who pursues the aim of imitation or originality? *With knowledge, the sewing of shoes may be sacred art too, but without it, a priest of contemporary art is worse than a cobbler.*" The last words were full of emphasis. Mr. Gurdjieff became silent, and A. said nothing.

The conversation had impressed me deeply; I felt how right A. had been in his warning that in order to listen to Mr. Gurdjieff more was required than just the wish to meet him.

My thought was working precisely and clearly. Thousands of questions rose in my mind, but none corresponded to the depth of what I had heard and so I remained silent.

I looked at Mr. Gurdjieff. He raised his head slowly and said: "I must go. Today it is enough. In half an hour there will be horses to take you to the train. About further plans you will learn from A.," and, turning to him, he added, "Take my place as host. Have breakfast with our guest. After taking him to the station, come back. . . . Well, goodbye."

A. crossed the room and pulled a cord concealed by an ottoman. A Persian rug hanging on the wall was drawn aside, revealing a huge window. Light from a clear, frosty winter's

morning filled the room. This took me by surprise: till that moment I had not thought of the hour.

"What time is it?" I exclaimed.

"Nearly nine," A. replied, putting out the lamps. He added,
smiling, "As you observe, time does not exist here."

II

God and microbe are the same system, the only difference is in the number of centers.

(Prieuré, April 3, 1923)

Our development is like that of a butterfly. We must "die and be reborn" as the egg dies and becomes a caterpillar; the caterpillar dies and becomes a chrysalis; the chrysalis dies and then the butterfly is born. It is a long process and the butterfly lives only a day or two. But the cosmic purpose is fulfilled. It is the same with man, we must destroy our buffers. Children have none; therefore we must become like little children. . . .

(Prieuré, June 2, 1922)

To someone who asked why we were born and why we die, Gurdjieff replied: You wish to know? To really know you must suffer. Can you suffer? You cannot suffer. You cannot suffer for one franc and to know a little you must suffer for one million francs. . . .

(Prieuré, August 12, 1924)

We listen to our own thoughts when learning, therefore we cannot hear new thoughts, only by new methods of listening and studying . . .

(London, February 13, 1922)

ESSENTUKI, ABOUT 1918

When speaking on different subjects, I have noticed how difficult it is to pass on one's understanding, even of the most ordinary subject and to a person well known to me. Our language is too poor for full and exact descriptions. Later I found that this lack of understanding between one man and another is a mathematically ordered phenomenon as precise as the multiplication table. It depends in general on the so-called "psyche" of the people concerned, and in particular on the state of their psyche at any given moment.

The truth of this law can be verified at every step. In order to be understood by another man, it is not only necessary for the speaker to know how to speak but for the listener to know how to listen. This is why I can say that if I were to speak in a way I consider exact, everybody here, with very few exceptions, would think I was crazy. But since at present I have to speak to my audience as it is, and my audience will have to listen to me, we must first establish the possibility of a common understanding.

In the course of our talk we must gradually mark the signposts of a productive conversation. All I wish to suggest now is that you try to look at things and phenomena around you, and especially at yourselves, from a point of view, from an angle, that may be different from what is usual or natural to you. Only to look, for to do more is possible only with the wish and cooperation of the listener, when the listener ceases to listen passively and begins to do, that is, when he moves into an active state.

Very often in conversation with people, one hears the direct or implied view that man as we meet with him in ordinary life could be regarded as almost the center of the universe, the "crown of creation," or at any rate that he is a large and important entity; that his possibilities are almost unlimited, his powers almost infinite. But even with such views there are a number of reservations: they say that, for this, exceptional conditions are necessary, special circumstances, inspiration, revelation and so on.

However, if we examine this conception of "man," we see at once that it is made up of features which belong not to one man but to a number of known or supposed separate individuals. We never meet such a man in real life, neither in the present nor as a historical personage in the past. For every man has his own weaknesses and if you look closely the mirage of greatness and power disintegrates.

But the most interesting thing is not that people clothe others in this mirage but that, owing to a peculiar feature of their own psyche, they transfer it to themselves, if not in its entirety, at least in part as a reflection. And so, although they are almost nonentities, they imagine themselves to be that collective type or not far removed from it.

But if a man knows how to be sincere with himself—not sincere as the word is usually understood, but mercilessly sincere —then, to the question "What are you?" he will not expect a comforting reply. So now, without waiting for you to come nearer to experiencing for yourselves what I am speaking about, I suggest that, in order to understand better what I mean, each of you should now ask himself the question "What am I?" I am certain that 95 percent of you will be puzzled by this question and will answer with another one: "What do you mean?"

And this will prove that a man has lived all his life without asking himself this question, has taken for granted, as axiomatic, that he is "something," even something very valuable, something he has never questioned. At the same time he is unable to explain to another what this something is, unable to convey even any idea of it, for he himself does not know what it is. Is the reason he does not know because, in fact, this "something" does not exist but is merely assumed to exist? Is it not strange that people pay so little attention to themselves in the sense of self-knowledge? Is it not strange with what dull complacency they shut their eyes to what they really are and spend their lives in the pleasant conviction that they represent something valuable? They fail to see the galling emptiness hidden behind the highly painted façade created by their self-delusion and do not realize that its value is purely conventional.

True, this is not always so. Not everyone looks at himself so superficially. There do exist enquiring minds, which long for the truth of the heart, seek it, strive to solve the problems set by life, try to penetrate to the essence of things and phenomena and to penetrate into themselves. If a man reasons and thinks soundly, no matter what path he follows in solving these problems, he must inevitably arrive back at himself, and begin with the solution of the problem of what he is himself and what his place is in the world around him. For without this knowledge, he will have no focal point in his search. Socrates' words "Know thyself" remain for all those who seek true knowledge and being.

I have just used a new word—"being." To make sure that we all understand the same thing by it, I shall have to say a few words in explanation.

We have just been questioning whether what a man thinks about himself corresponds to what he is in reality, and you have asked yourselves what you are. Here is a doctor, there an engineer, there an artist. Are they in reality what we think they are? Can we treat the personality of each one as identical with his profession, with the experience which that profession, or the preparation for it, has given him?

Every man comes into the world like a clean sheet of paper; and then the people and circumstances around him begin vying with each other to dirty this sheet and to cover it with writing. Education, the formation of morals, information we call knowledge—all feelings of duty, honor, conscience and so on—enter here. And they all claim that the methods adopted for grafting these shoots known as man's "personality" to the trunk are immutable and infallible. Gradually the sheet is dirtied, and the dirtier with so-called "knowledge" the sheet becomes, the cleverer the man is considered to be. The more writing there is in the place called "duty," the more honest the possessor is said to be; and so it is with everything. And the dirty sheet itself, seeing that people consider its "dirt" as merit, considers it valuable. This is an example of what we call "man," to which we often even add such words as talent and genius. Yet our "genius" will have his mood spoiled for the whole day if he does not find his slippers beside his bed when he wakes up in the morning.

A man is not free either in his manifestations or in his life. He cannot be what he wishes to be and what he thinks he is. He is not like his picture of himself, and the words "man, the crown of creation" do not apply to him.

"Man"—this is a proud term, but we must ask ourselves what kind of man? Not the man, surely, who is irritated at trifles, who gives his attention to petty matters and gets involved in everything around him. To have the right to call himself a man, he must be a man; and this "being" comes only through self-knowledge and work on oneself in the directions that become clear through self-knowledge.

Have you ever tried to watch yourself mentally when your attention has not been set on some definite problem for concentration? I suppose most of you are familiar with this, although perhaps only a few have systematically watched it in themselves. You are no doubt aware of the way we think by chance association, when our thought strings disconnected scenes and memories together, when everything that falls within the field of our consciousness, or merely touches it lightly, calls up these chance associations in our thought. The string of thoughts seems to go on uninterruptedly, weaving together fragments of representations of former perceptions, taken from different recordings in our memories. And these recordings turn and unwind while our thinking apparatus deftly weaves its threads of thought continuously from this material. The records of our feelings revolve in the same way—pleasant and unpleasant, joy and sorrow, laughter and irritation, pleasure and pain, sympathy and antipathy. You hear yourself praised and you are pleased; someone reproves you and your mood is spoiled. Something new captures your interest and instantly makes you forget what interested you just as much the moment before. Gradually your interest attaches you to the new thing to such an extent that you sink into it from head to foot; suddenly you do not possess it any more, you have disappeared, you are bound to and dissolved in this thing; in fact it possesses you, it has captivated you, and this infatuation, this capacity for being captivated is, under many different guises, a property of each one of us. This binds us and prevents our being free. By the same token it takes away our strength and our time, leaving us no possibility of being objective and free —two essential qualities for anyone who decides to follow the way of self-knowledge.

We must strive for freedom if we strive for self-knowledge. The task of self-knowledge and of further self-development is of such importance and seriousness, it demands such intensity of effort, that to attempt it any old way and amongst other things is impossible. The person who undertakes this task must put it first in his life, which is not so long that he can afford to squander it on trifles.

What can allow a man to spend his time profitably in his search, if not freedom from every kind of attachment?

Freedom and seriousness. Not the kind of seriousness which looks out from under knitted brows with pursed lips, carefully restrained gestures and words filtered through the teeth, but the kind of seriousness that means determination and persistence in the search, intensity and constancy in it, so that a man, even when resting, continues with his main task.

Ask yourselves—are you free? Many are inclined to answer "yes," if they are relatively secure in a material sense and do not have to worry about the morrow, if they depend on no one for their livelihood or in the choice of their conditions of life. But is this freedom? Is it only a question of external conditions?

You have plenty of money, let us say. You live in luxury and enjoy general respect and esteem. The people who run your well-organized business are absolutely honest and devoted to you. In a word, you have a very good life. Perhaps you think so yourself and consider yourself wholly free, for after all your time is your own. You are a patron of the arts, you settle world problems over a cup of coffee and you may even be interested in the development of hidden spiritual powers. Problems of the spirit are not foreign to you and you are at home among philosophical ideas. You are educated and well read. Having some erudition in many fields, you are known as a clever man, for you find your way easily in all sorts of pursuits; you are an example of a cultured man. In short, you are to be envied.

In the morning you wake up under the influence of an unpleasant dream. The slightly depressed mood disappeared but has left its trace in a kind of lassitude and uncertainty of movement. You go to the mirror to brush your hair and by accident drop your hairbrush. You pick it up and just as you have dusted it off, you drop it again. This time you pick it up with a shade of impatience and because of that you drop it a third time. You try to grab it in midair but instead, it flies at the mirror. In vain you jump to catch it. Smash! . . . a star-shaped cluster of cracks appears in the antique mirror you were so proud of. Hell! The records of discontent begin to turn. You need to vent your annoyance on someone. Finding that your servant has forgotten to put the newspaper beside your morning coffee, your cup of patience overflows and you decide you can no longer stand the wretched man in the house.

Now it is time for you to go out. Taking advantage of the fine day, your destination not being far away, you decide to walk while your car follows slowly behind. The bright sun somewhat mollifies you. Your attention is attracted to a crowd that has gathered around a man lying unconscious on the pavement. With the help of the onlookers the porter puts him into a cab and he is driven off to the hospital. Notice how the strangely familiar face of the driver is connected in your associations and reminds you of the accident you had last year. You were returning home from a gay birthday party. What a delicious cake they had there! This servant of yours who forgot your morning paper ruined your breakfast. Why not make up for it now? After all, cake and coffee are extremely important! Here is the fashionable café you sometimes go to with your friends. But why have you remembered about the accident? You had surely almost forgotten about the morning's unpleasantness. . . . And now, do your cake and coffee really taste so good?

You see the two ladies at the next table. What a charming blonde! She glances at you and whispers to her companion, "That's the sort of man I like."

Surely none of your troubles are worth wasting time on or getting upset about. Need one point out how your mood changed from the moment you met the blonde and how it lasted while you were with her? You return home humming a gay tune and even the broken mirror only provokes a smile. But what about the business you went out for in the morning? You have only just remembered it . . . that's clever! Still, it does not matter. You can telephone. You lift the receiver and the operator gives you the wrong number. You ring again and get the same number. Some man says sharply that he is sick of you—you say it is not your fault, an altercation follows and you are surprised to learn that you are a fool and an idiot, and that if you call again . . . The rumpled carpet under your foot irritates you, and you should hear the tone of voice in which you reprove the servant who is handing you a letter. The letter is from a man you respect and whose good opinion you value. The contents of the letter are so flattering to you that your irritation gradually dies down and is replaced by the pleasantly embarrassed feeling that flattery arouses. You finish reading it in a most amiable mood.

I could continue this picture of your day—you free man. Perhaps you think I have been exaggerating. No, this is a true scenario taken from life.

This was a day in the life of a man well known both at home and abroad, a day reconstructed and described by him that same evening as a vivid example of associative thinking and feeling. Tell me where is the freedom when people and things possess a man to such an extent that he forgets his mood, his business and himself? In a man who is subject to such variation can there be any serious attitude toward his search?

You understand better now that a man need not necessarily be what he appears to be, that the question is not one of external circumstances and facts but of the inner structure of a man and of his attitude toward these facts. But perhaps this is only true for his associations; with regard to things he "knows" about, perhaps the situation is different.

But I ask you, if for some reason each of you was unable to put your knowledge to practical use for several years, how much would remain? Would this not be like having materials which in time dry up and evaporate? Remember the comparison with a clean sheet of paper. And indeed in the course of our life we are learning something the whole time, and we call the results of this learning "knowledge." And in spite of this knowledge, do we not often prove to be ignorant, remote from real life and therefore ill-adapted to it? We are half-educated like tadpoles, or more often simply "educated" people with a little information about many things but all of it woolly and inadequate. Indeed it is merely information. We cannot call it knowledge, since knowledge is an inalienable property of a man; it cannot be more and it cannot be less. For a man "knows" only when he himself "is" that knowledge. As for your convictions—have you never known them to change? Are they not also subject to fluctuation like everything else in us? Would it not be more accurate to call them opinions rather than convictions, dependent as much on our mood as on our information or perhaps simply on the state of our digestion at a given moment?

Every one of you is a rather uninteresting example of an animated automaton. You think that a "soul," and even a "spirit," is necessary to do what you do and live as you live. But perhaps it is enough to have a key for winding up the spring of your mechanism. Your daily portions of food help to wind you up and renew the purposeless antics of associations again and again. From this background separate thoughts are selected and you attempt to connect them into a whole and pass them off as valuable and as your own. We also pick out feelings and sensations, moods and experiences and out of all this we create the mirage of an inner life, call ourselves conscious and reasoning beings, talk about God, about eternity, about eternal life and other higher matters; we speak about everything imaginable, judge and discuss, define and evaluate, but we omit to speak about ourselves and about our own real objective value, for we are all convinced that if there is anything lacking in us, we can acquire it.

If in what I have said I have succeeded even to a small extent in making clear in what chaos is the being we call man, you will be able to answer for yourselves the question of what he lacks and what he can obtain if he remains as he is, what of value he can add to the value he himself represents.

I have already said that there are people who hunger and thirst for truth. If they examine the problems of life and are sincere with themselves, they soon become convinced that it is not possible to live as they have lived and to be what they have been until now; that a way out of this situation is essential and that a man can develop his hidden capacities and powers only by cleaning his machine of the dirt that has clogged it in the course of his life. But in order to undertake this cleaning in a rational way, he has to see what needs to be cleaned, where and how; but to see this for himself is almost impossible. In order to see anything of this one has to look from the outside; and for this mutual help is necessary.

If you remember the example I gave of identification, you will see how blind a man is when he identifies with his moods, feelings and thoughts. But is our dependence on things only limited to what can be observed at first glance? These things are so much in relief that they cannot help catching the eye. You remember how we spoke about people's characters, roughly dividing them into good and bad? As a man gets to know himself, he continually finds new areas of his mechani- calness—let us call it automatism—domains where his will, his "I wish," has no power, areas not subject to him, so confused and subtle that it is impossible to find his way about in them without the help and the authoritative guidance of someone who knows.

This briefly is the state of things in the realm of self-knowl- edge: in order to do you must know; but to know you must find out how to know. We cannot find this out by ourselves.

Besides self-knowledge, there is another aspect of the search —self-development. Let us see how things stand there. It is clear that a man left to his own devices cannot wring out of his little finger the knowledge of how to develop and, still less, exactly what to develop in himself.

Gradually, by meeting people who are searching, by talking

to them and by reading relevant books, a man becomes drawn into the sphere of questions concerning self-development.

But what may he meet here? First of all an abyss of the most unpardonable charlatanism, based entirely on the greed for making money by hoaxing gullible people who are seeking a way out of their spiritual impotence. But before a man learns to divide the wheat from the tares, a long time must elapse and perhaps the urge itself to find the truth will flicker and go out in him, or will become morbidly perverted and his blunted flair may lead him into such a labyrinth that the path out of it, figuratively speaking, will lead straight to the devil. If a man succeeds in getting out of this first swamp, he may fall into a new quagmire of pseudo-knowledge. In that case truth will be served up in such an indigestible and vague form that it produces the impression of a pathological delirium. He will be shown ways and means of developing hidden powers and capacities which he is promised, if he is persistent, will without much trouble give him power and domain over everything, including animate creatures, inert matter and the elements. All these systems, based on a variety of theories, are extraordinarily alluring, no doubt precisely because of their vagueness. They have a particular attraction for the half-educated, those who are half-instructed in positivist knowledge.

In view of the fact that most questions studied from the point of view of esoteric and occult theories often go beyond the limits of data accessible to modern science, these theories often look down on it. Although on the one hand they give positivist science its due, on the other, they belittle its importance and leave the impression that science is not only a failure but even worse.

What is the use then of going to the university, of studying and straining over official textbooks, if theories of this kind enable one to look down on all other learning and to pass judgment on scientific questions?

But there is one important thing the study of such theories

does not give; it does not engender objectivity in questions of knowledge, less so even than science. Indeed it tends to blur a man's brain and to diminish his capacity for reasoning and thinking soundly, and leads him toward psychopathy. This is the effect of such theories on the half-educated who take them for authentic revelation. But their effect is not very different on scientists themselves, who may have been affected, however slightly, by the poison of discontent with existing things. Our thinking machine possesses the capacity to be convinced of anything you like, provided it is repeatedly and persistently influenced in the required direction. A thing that may appear absurd to start with will in the end become rationalized, provided it is repeated sufficiently often and with sufficient conviction. And, just as one type will repeat ready-made words which have stuck in his mind, so a second type will find intricate proofs and paradoxes to explain what he says. But both are equally to be pitied. All these theories offer assertions which, like dogmas, usually cannot be verified. Or in any case they cannot be verified by the means available to us.

Then methods and ways of self-development are suggested which are said to lead to a state in which their assertions can be verified. There can be no objection to this in principle. But the consistent practice of these methods may lead the over-zealous seeker to highly undesirable results. A man who accepts occult theories and believes himself knowledgeable in this sphere will not be able to resist the temptation to put into practice the knowledge of the methods he has gained in his research, that is, he will pass from knowledge to action. Perhaps he will act with circumspection, avoiding methods which from his point of view are risky, and applying the more reliable and authentic ways; perhaps he will observe with the greatest of care. All the same, the temptation to apply them and the insistence on the necessity for doing so, as well as the emphasis laid on the miraculous nature of the results and the concealment of their dark sides, will lead a man to try them.

Perhaps, in trying them, a man will find methods which are harmless for him. Perhaps, in applying them, he will even get something from them. In general, all the methods for self-development which are offered, whether for verification, as a means, or as an end, are often contradictory and incomprehensible. Dealing as they do with such an intricate, little-known machine as the human organism and with that side of our life closely connected with it which we call our psyche, the least mistake in carrying them out, the smallest error or excess of pressure can lead to irreparable damage to the machine.

It is indeed lucky if a man escapes from this morass more or less intact. Unfortunately very many of those who are engaged in the development of spiritual powers and capacities end their career in a lunatic asylum or ruin their health and psyche to such a degree that they become complete invalids, unable to adapt to life. Their ranks are swelled by those who are attracted to pseudo-occultism out of a longing for anything miraculous and mysterious. There are also those exceptionally weak-willed individuals who are failures in life and who, out of considerations of personal gain, dream of developing in themselves the power and the ability to subjugate others. And finally there are people who are simply looking for variety in life, for ways of forgetting their sorrows, of finding distraction from the boredom of the daily round and of escaping its conflicts.

As their hopes of attaining the qualities they counted on begin to dwindle, it is easy for them to fall into intentional charlatanism. I remember a classic example. A certain seeker after psychic power, a man who was well off, well read, who had traveled widely in his search for anything miraculous, ended by going bankrupt and became at the same time disillusioned in all his researches.

Looking for another means of livelihood, he hit on the idea of making use of the pseudo-knowledge on which he had spent so much money and energy. No sooner said than done. He wrote a book, bearing one of those titles that adorn the covers of occult books, something like *A Course in Development of the Hidden Forces in Man.*

This course was written in seven lectures and represented a short encyclopedia of secret methods for developing magnetism, hypnotism, telepathy, clairvoyance, clairaudience, escape into the astral realm, levitation and other alluring capacities. The course was well advertised, put on sale at an exceedingly high price, although in the end an appreciable discount (up to 95 percent) was offered to the more persistent or parsimonious customers on condition that they recommend it to their friends.

Owing to the general interest in such matters, the success of the course exceeded all the expectations of its compiler. Soon he began to receive letters from purchasers in enthusiastic, reverent and deferential tones, addressing him as "dear teacher" and "wise mentor" and expressing deepest gratitude for the wonderful exposition and most valuable instruction which gave them the possibility of developing various occult capacities remarkably quickly.

These letters made a considerable collection and each of them surprised him until there at last came a letter informing him that with the help of his course someone had, in about a month, become able to levitate. This indeed overran the cup of his astonishment.

Here are his actual words: "I am astonished at the absurdity of things that happen. I, who wrote the course, have no very clear idea of the nature of the phenomena I am teaching. Yet these idiots not only find their way about in this gibberish but even learn something from it and now some superidiot has even learned to fly. It is, of course, all nonsense. He can go to hell. . . . Soon they will put him into a straitjacket. It will serve him right. We are much better off without such fools."

Occultists, do you appreciate the argument of this author of one of the textbooks on psychodevelopment? In this case, it is possible that somebody might accidentally learn something, for often a man, though ignorant himself, can speak with cu-

rious correctness about various things, without knowing how
he does it. At the same time, of course, he also talks such nonsense that any truths he may have expressed are completely
buried and it is utterly impossible to dig the pearl of truth out
of the muckheap of every kind of nonsense.

"Why this strange capacity?" you may ask. The reason is
very simple. As I have already said, we have no knowledge of
our own, that is, knowledge given by life itself, knowledge that
cannot be taken away from us. All our knowledge, which is
merely information, may be valuable or worthless. In absorb-
ing it like a sponge, we can easily repeat and talk about it logically and convincingly, while understanding nothing about it.
It is equally easy for us to lose it, for it is not ours but has been
poured into us like some liquid poured into a vessel. Crumbs
of truth are scattered everywhere; and those who know and
understand can see and marvel how close people live to the
truth, yet how blind they are and powerless to penetrate it.
But in searching for it, it is far better not to venture at all into
the dark labyrinths of human stupidity and ignorance than to
go there alone. For without the guidance and explanations of
someone who knows, a man at every step, without noticing it,
may suffer a strain, a dislocation of his machine, after which he
would have to spend a great deal more on its repair than he
spent damaging it.

What can you think of a solid individual who says of himself
that "he is a man of perfect meekness and that his behavior is
not under the jurisdiction of those around him, since he lives
on a mental plane to which standards of physical life cannot
be applied"? Actually, his behavior should long ago have been
the subject of study by a psychiatrist. This is a man who conscientiously and persistently "works" on himself for hours
daily, that is, he applies all his efforts to deepening and
strengthening further the psychological twist, which is already
so serious that I am convinced that he will soon be in an in-
sane asylum.

I could quote hundreds of examples of wrongly directed

search and where it leads. I could tell you the names of well-known people in public life who have become deranged through occultism and who live in our midst and astonish us by their eccentricities. I could tell you the exact method that deranged them, in what realm they "worked" and "developed" themselves and how these affected their psychological makeup and why.

But this question could form the subject of a long and separate conversation so, for lack of time, I will not permit myself to dwell on it now.

The more a man studies the obstacles and deceptions which lie in wait for him at every step in this realm, the more convinced he becomes that it is impossible to travel the path of self-development on the chance instructions of chance people, or the kind of information culled from reading and casual talk.

At the same time he gradually sees more clearly—first a feeble glimmer, then the clear light of truth which has illumined mankind throughout the ages. The beginnings of initiation are lost in the darkness of time, where the long chain of epochs unfolds. Great cultures and civilizations loom up, dimly arising from cults and mysteries, ever changing, disappearing and reappearing.

The Great Knowledge is handed on in succession from age to age, from people to people, from race to race. The great centers of initiation in India, Assyria, Egypt, Greece, illumine the world with a bright light. The revered names of the great initiates, the living bearers of the truth, are handed on reverently from generation to generation. Truth is fixed by means of symbolical writings and legends and is transmitted to the mass of people for preservation in the form of customs and ceremonies, in oral traditions, in memorials, in sacred art through the invisible quality in dance, music, sculpture and various rituals. It is communicated openly after a definite trial to those who seek it and is preserved by oral transmission in the chain of those who know. After a certain time has elapsed, the centers of initiation die out one after another, and the ancient knowledge departs through underground channels into the deep, hiding from the eyes of the seekers.

The bearers of this knowledge also hide, becoming unknown to those around them, but they do not cease to exist. From time to time separate streams break through to the surface, showing that somewhere deep down in the interior, even in our day, there flows the powerful ancient stream of true knowledge of being.

To break through to this stream, to find it—this is the task and the aim of the search; for, having found it, a man can entrust himself boldly to the way by which he intends to go; then there only remains "to know" in order "to be" and "to do." On this way a man will not be entirely alone; at difficult moments he will receive support and guidance, for all who follow this way are connected by an uninterrupted chain.

Perhaps the only positive result of all wanderings in the winding paths and tracks of occult research will be that, if a man preserves the capacity for sound judgment and thought, he will evolve that special faculty of discrimination which can be called flair. He will discard the ways of psychopathy and error and will persistently search for true ways. And here, as in self-knowledge, the principle which I have already quoted holds good: "In order to do, it is necessary to know; but in order to know, it is necessary to find out how to know."

To a man who is searching with all his being, with all his inner self, comes the unfailing conviction that to find out how to know in order to do is possible only by finding a guide with experience and knowledge, who will take on his spiritual guidance and become his teacher.

And it is here that a man's flair is more important than anywhere else. He chooses a guide for himself. It is of course an indispensable condition that he choose as a guide a man who knows, or else all meaning of choice is lost. Who can tell where a guide who does not know may lead a man?

Every seeker dreams of a guide who knows, dreams about

him but seldom asks himself objectively and sincerely—is he worthy of being guided? Is he ready to follow the way?

Go out one clear starlit night to some open space and look up at the sky, at those millions of worlds over your head. Remember that perhaps on each of them swarm billions of beings, similar to you or perhaps superior to you in their organization. Look at the Milky Way. The earth cannot even be called a grain of sand in this infinity. It dissolves and vanishes, and with it, you. Where are you? And is what you want simply madness?

Before all these worlds ask yourself what are your aims and hopes, your intentions and means of fulfilling them, the demands that may be made upon you and your preparedness to meet them.

A long and difficult journey is before you; you are preparing for a strange and unknown land. The way is infinitely long. You do not know if rest will be possible on the way nor where it will be possible. You should be prepared for the worst. Take all the necessities for the journey with you.

Try to forget nothing, for afterwards it will be too late and there will be no time to go back for what has been forgotten, to rectify the mistake. Weigh up your strength. Is it sufficient for the whole journey? How soon can you start?

Remember that if you spend longer on the way you will need to carry proportionately more supplies, and this will delay you further both on the way and in your preparations for it. Yet every minute is precious. Once having decided to go, there is no use wasting time.

Do not reckon on trying to come back. This experiment may cost you very dear. The guide undertakes only to take you there and, if you wish to turn back, he is not obliged to return with you. You will be left to yourself, and woe to you if you weaken or forget the way—you will never get back. And even if you remember the way, the question still remains—will you return safe and sound? For many unpleasantnesses await the lonely traveler who is not familiar with the way and the customs which prevail there. Bear in mind that your sight has the property of presenting distant objects as though they were near. Beguiled by the nearness of the aim toward which you strive, blinded by its beauty and ignorant of the measure of your own strength, you will not notice the obstacles on the way; you will not see the numerous ditches across the path. In a green meadow covered with luxuriant flowers, in the thick grass, a deep precipice is hidden. It is very easy to stumble and fall over it if your eyes are not concentrated on the step you are taking.

Do not forget to concentrate all your attention on the nearest sector of the way—do not concern yourself about far aims if you do not wish to fall over the precipice.

Yet do not forget your aim. Remember it the whole time and keep up in yourself an active endeavor toward it, so as not to lose the right direction. And once you have started, be observant; what you have passed through remains behind and will not appear again; so if you fail to notice it at the time, you never will notice it.

Do not be overcurious nor waste time on things that attract your attention but are not worth it. Time is precious and should not be wasted on things which have no direct relation to your aim.

Remember where you are and why you are here.

Do not protect yourselves and remember that no effort is made in vain.

And now you can set out on the way.

For an exact study, an exact language is needed. But our ordinary language in which we speak, set forth what we know and understand, and write books in ordinary life, does not do for even a small amount of exact speech. An inexact speech cannot serve an exact knowledge. The words composing our language are too wide, too foggy and indefinite, while the meaning put into them is too arbitrary and variable. Every man who pronounces any word always attaches this or that shade of meaning to it by his imagination, exaggerates or puts forward this or that side of it, sometimes concentrating all the significance of the word on a single feature of the object, that is, designating by this word not all the attributes but those chance external ones which first spring to his notice. Another man speaking with the first attaches to the same word another shade of meaning, takes this word in another sense, which is often exactly the opposite. If a third man joins the conversation, he again puts into the same word his own meaning. And if ten people speak, every one of them once more gives his own meaning, and the same word has ten meanings. And men speaking in this way think that they can understand each other, that they can transfer their thoughts one to another.

It can be said with full confidence that the language in

which contemporary men speak is so imperfect that whatever they speak about, especially on scientific matters, they can never be sure that they call the same ideas by the same words.

On the contrary, one can say almost certainly that they understand every word differently and, while appearing to speak about the same subject, in practice speak about quite different things. Moreover, for every man the meaning of his own words and the meaning which he puts into them changes in accordance with his own thoughts and humors, with the images which he associates at the moment with the words, as well as with what and how his interlocutor speaks, for by an involuntary imitation or contradiction he can involuntarily change the meaning of his words. In addition, nobody is able to define exactly what he means by this or that word, or whether this meaning is constant or subject to change, how, why and for what reason.

If several men speak, everyone speaks in his own way, and no one of them understands another. A professor reads a lecture, a scholar writes a book, and their audience and readers listen to, and read, not them but combinations of the authors' words and their own thoughts, notions, humors and emotions of the given moment.

The people of today are, to a certain degree, conscious of the instability of their language. Among the diverse branches of science every one of them works out its own terminology, its own nomenclature and language. In philosophy attempts are made, before using any word, to make clear in what sense it is taken; but however much people nowadays try to establish a constant meaning of words, they have failed in it so far. Every writer fixes his own terminology, changes the terminology of his predecessors, contradicts his own terminology; in short, everyone contributes his share to the general confusion.

This teaching points out the cause of this. Our words have not and cannot have any constant meaning, and to indicate at every word the meaning and the particular shade which we attach to this word, that is, the relations in which it is taken by us, we have in the first place no means; and secondly we do not aim at this; on the contrary, we invariably wish to establish our constant meaning for a word and to take it always in that sense, which is obviously impossible, as one and the same word used at different times and in various relations has different meanings.

Our wrong use of words and the qualities of the words themselves have made them unreliable instruments of an exact speech and an exact knowledge, not to mention the fact that for many notions accessible to our reason we have neither words nor expressions.

The language of numbers alone can serve for an exact expression of thought and knowledge; but the language of numbers is applied only to designate and compare quantities. But things do not differ only in size, and their definition from the point of view of quantities is not sufficient for an exact knowledge and analysis. We do not know how to apply the language of numbers to the attributes of things. If we knew how to do it and could designate all the qualities of things by numbers in relation to some immutable number, this would be an exact language.

The teaching whose principles we are going to expound here has as one of its tasks the bringing of our thinking nearer to an exact mathematical designation of things and events and the giving to men of the possibility of understanding themselves and each other.

If we take any of the most commonly used words and try to see what a varied meaning these words have according to who uses them and in what connection, we shall see why men have no power of expressing their thoughts exactly and why everything men say and think is so unstable and contradictory. Apart from the variety of meanings which every word can have, this confusion and contradiction are caused by the fact that men never render any account to themselves of the sense in which they take this or that word and only wonder why others do not understand it although it is so clear to themselves. For example, if we say the word "world" in front of ten hearers, every one of them will understand the word in his own way. If men knew how to catch and write down their thoughts themselves, they would see that they had no ideas connected with the word "world" but that merely a well-known word and an accustomed sound was uttered, the significance of which is supposed to be known. It is as if everybody hearing this word said to himself: "Ah, the 'world,' I know what it is." As a matter of fact he does not really know at all. But the word is familiar, and therefore no such question and answer occur to him. It is just accepted. A question comes only in respect of new unknown words and then the man tends to substitute for the unknown word a known one. He calls this "understanding."

If we now ask the man what he understands by the word "world," he will be perplexed by such a question. Usually, when he hears or uses the word "world" in conversation, he does not think at all about what it means, having decided once and for all that he knows and that everybody knows. Now for the first time he sees that he does not know and that he has never thought about it; but he will not be able to and will not know how to rest with the thought of his ignorance. Men are not capable enough of observing and not sufficiently sincere with themselves to do so. He will soon recover himself, that is, he will very quickly deceive himself; and remembering or composing in haste a definition of the word "world" from some familiar source of knowledge or thought, or the first definition of someone else's which enters his head, he will express it as his own understanding of the meaning of the word, though in fact he has never thought about the word "world" in this way and does not know how he has thought.

The man interested in astronomy will say that the "world" consists of an enormous number of suns surrounded by planets, placed at immeasurable distances from one another and composing what we call the Milky Way, beyond which are still further distances and, beyond the limits of investigation, other stars and other worlds may be supposed to lie.

He who is interested in physics will speak about the world of vibrations and electric discharges, about the theory of energy, or perhaps about the likeness of the world of atoms and electrons to the world of suns and planets.

The man inclined to philosophy will begin to speak about the unreality and illusory character of the whole visible world created in time and space by our feeling and senses. He will say that the world of atoms and electrons, the earth with its mountains and seas, its vegetable and animal life, men and towns, the sun, the stars, and the Milky Way, all these are the world of phenomena, a deceptive, untrue and illusory world, created by our own conception. Beyond this world, beyond the limits of our knowledge, there lies a world, incomprehensible for us, of noumena—a shadow, a reflection of which is the phenomenal world.

The man acquainted with the modern theory of many-dimensional space will say that the world is usually regarded as an infinite three-dimensional sphere, but that in reality the three-dimensional world, as such, cannot exist, and represents only an imaginary section of another, a four-dimensional world, from which all our events come and where they go.

A man whose world concept is built on the dogma of religion will say that the world is the creation of God and depends upon God's will, that beyond the visible world, where our life is short and dependent on circumstances or accident, an invisible world exists where life is eternal and where man will receive a reward or punishment for everything he has done in this life.

A theosophist will say that the astral world does not embrace the visible world as a whole, but that seven worlds exist penetrating one another mutually and composed of more or less subtle matter.

A Russian peasant, or a peasant of some Eastern countries, will say that the world is the village community of which he is a member. This world is nearest to him. He even addresses his fellow villagers at general meetings by calling them the "world."

All these definitions of the word "world" have their merits and defects: their chief defect consists in that each of them excludes its opposite, while all picture one side of the world and examine it only from one point of view. A correct definition will be such as would combine all the separate understandings, showing the place of each and at the same time giving, in each case, the possibility of stating about which side of the world the man speaks, from which point of view and in which relation.

This teaching says that if the question of what the world is were approached in the right way, we could establish quite accurately what we understand by this word. And this definition of a right understanding would include in itself all views upon the world and all approaches to the question. Having thus agreed on such a definition, men would be able to understand one another when speaking about the world. Only starting from such a definition can one speak about the world.

But how to find this definition? The teaching points out that the first thing is to come to the question as simply as possible; that is, to take the most commonly used expressions with which we speak about the world and to consider about which world we speak. In other words, to look at our own relation to the world and take the world in its relation to ourselves. We shall see that, speaking of the world, we most often speak of the earth, of the terrestrial globe, or rather of the surface of the terrestrial globe, that is, just the world in which we live.

If we now look at the relation of the earth to the universe, we shall see that on the one hand the earth's satellite is included in the sphere of its influence, while on the other the earth enters as a component part into the planetary world of our solar system. The earth is one of the small planets turning round the sun. The mass of the earth forms an almost negligible fraction compared with the whole mass of planets of the solar system, and the planets exert a very great influence on the life of the earth and on all existing and living organisms—a far greater influence than our science imagines. The life of individual men, of collective groups, of humanity, depends upon planetary influences in very many things. The planets also live, as we live upon the earth. But the planetary world in its turn enters into the solar system, and enters as a very unimportant part because the mass of all the planets put together is many times less than the mass of the sun.

The world of the sun is also a world in which we live. The sun in turn enters into the world of stars, in the enormous accumulation of suns forming the Milky Way.

The starry world is also a world in which we live. Taken as a whole, even according to the definition of modern astronomers, the starry world seems to represent a separate entity having a definite form, surrounded by space beyond the limits of which scientific investigation cannot penetrate. But astronomy supposes that at immeasurable distances from our starry world other accumulations may exist. If we accept this supposition, we shall say that our starry world enters as a component part into the total quantity of these worlds. This accumulation of worlds of the "All Worlds" is also a world in which we live.

Science cannot look further, but philosophical thought will see the ultimate principle lying beyond all the worlds, that is, the Absolute, known in Hindu terminology as Brahman.

All that has been said about the world can be represented by a simple diagram. Let us designate the earth by a small circle and mark it with the letter A. Inside the circle A let us place a smaller circle, representing the moon, and let us mark it with the letter B. Round the circle of the earth let us draw a larger circle showing the world into which the earth enters and let us mark it with the letter C. Round this let us draw the circle representing the sun and mark it with the letter D. Then round this circle again a circle representing the starry world which we shall mark with the letter E, and then the circle of all worlds which we mark with the letter F. The circle F we shall enclose in the circle G designating the philosophical principle of all things, the Absolute.

The diagram will appear as seven concentric circles. Keeping this diagram in view, a man in pronouncing the word "world" will always be able to define exactly which world he is speaking about and in what relation to this world he stands.

As we shall explain later, the same diagram will help us to understand and combine together the astronomical definition of the world, the philosophical, physical and physico-chemical definitions as well as the mathematical one (the world of many dimensions), and the theosophical (worlds interpenetrating one another) and others.

This also makes clear why men speaking about the world can never understand one another. We live at one and the same time in six worlds, just as we live on a floor of such and such a house, in such and such a street, in such and such a town, such and such a state, and such and such a part of the world.

If a man speaks about the place where he lives without indicating whether he refers to the floor or the town or the part of the world, he certainly will not be understood by his interlocutors. But men always speak in this way about anything having no practical importance; and, as we saw in the example of the "world," they designate too readily by a single word a series of notions which are related to one another as a negligible part is related to an enormous whole, and so on. But an exact speech should point out always and quite exactly in what relation each notion is taken and what it includes in itself. That is, of what parts it consists and into what it enters as a component part.

Logically it is intelligible and inevitable, but unfortunately it never comes to pass if only for the reason that men very often do not know, and don't know how to find, the different parts and the relations of the given notion.

The making clear of the relativity of every notion, taking it not in the sense of the general abstract idea that everything in the world is relative but indicating exactly in what and how it relates to the rest, is an important part of the principles of this teaching.

If we now take the notion "man," we shall again see the misunderstanding of this word, we shall see that the same contradictions are put into it. Everybody uses this word and thinks he understands what "man" means: but as a matter of fact, each one understands in his own way, and all in different ways.

The learnèd naturalist sees in man a perfected breed of monkey and defines man by the construction of the teeth and so on.

The religious man, who believes in God and the future life, sees in man his immortal soul confined in a perishable terrestrial envelope, which is surrounded by temptations and leads man into danger.

The political economist considers man as a producing and consuming entity.

All these views seem entirely opposed to one another, contradicting one another and having no points of contact with one another. Moreover, the question is further complicated by the fact that we see among men many differences, so great and so sharply defined that it often seems strange to use the general term "man" for these beings of such different categories.

And if, in the face of all this, we ask ourselves what man is, we shall see that we cannot answer the question—we do not know what is man.

Neither anatomically, physiologically, psychologically nor economically do the definitions suffice here, as they relate to all men equally, without allowing us to distinguish differences which we see in man.

Our teaching points out that our store of information about man would be quite sufficient for the purpose of determining what man is. But we don't know how to approach the matter simply. We ourselves complicate and entangle the question too much.

Man is the being who can "do," says this teaching. To do means to act consciously and according to one's will. And we must recognize that we cannot find any more complete definition of man.

Animals differ from plants by their power of locomotion. And although a mollusc attached to a rock, and also certain seaweeds capable of moving against the current, seem to violate this law, yet the law is quite true—a plant can neither hunt for food, avoid a shock nor hide itself from its pursuer.

Man differs from the animal by his capacity for conscious action, his capacity for doing. We cannot deny this, and we see that this definition satisfies all requirements. It makes it possible to single out man from a series of other beings not possessing the power of conscious action, and at the same time according to the degree of consciousness in his actions.

Without any exaggeration we can say that all the differences which strike us among men can be reduced to the differences in the consciousness of their actions. Men seem to us to vary so much just because the actions of some of them are, according to our opinion, deeply conscious, while the actions of others are so unconscious that they even seem to surpass the unconsciousness of stones, which at least react rightly to external phenomena. The question is complicated by the mere fact that often one and the same man shows us, side by side with what appear to us entirely conscious actions of will, other quite unconscious animal-mechanical reactions. In virtue of this, man appears to us to be an extraordinarily complicated being. This teaching denies this complication and puts before us a very difficult task in connection with man. Man is he who can "do" but among ordinary men, as well as among those who are considered extraordinary, there is no one who can "do." In their case, everything from beginning to end is "done," there is nothing they can "do."

In personal, family and social life, in politics, science, art, philosophy and religion, everything from beginning to end is "done," nobody can "do" anything. If two persons, beginning a conversation about man, agree to call him a being capable of action, of "doing," they will always understand one another. Certainly they will make sufficiently clear what "doing" means. In order to "do," a very high degree of being and of knowledge is necessary. Ordinary men do not even understand what "doing" means because, in their own case and in everything around them, everything is always "done" and has always been "done." And yet man can "do."

A man who sleeps cannot "do." With him everything is done in sleep. Sleep is understood here not in the literal sense of our organic sleep, but in the sense of a state of associative existence. First of all he must awake. Having awakened, he will see that as he is he cannot "do." He will have to die voluntarily. When he is dead he may be born. But the being who has just been born must grow and learn. When he has grown and knows, then he will "do."

If we analyze what has been said about man, we see that the first half of what has been said, that is, that man cannot "do" anything and that everything is "done" in him, coincides with what positive science says about man. According to the positivist view, man is a very complicated organism which has developed, by the way of evolution, from the simplest organism and is capable of reacting in a very complicated manner to external impressions. This capacity for reaction in man is so complicated, and the answering movements may be so remote from the causes which called them forth and conditioned them, that a man's actions, or at least a part of them, seem to a naive observer to be quite spontaneous and independent.

As a matter of fact, man is not capable of even the smallest independent or spontaneous action. The whole of him is nothing but the result of external influences. Man is a process, a transmitting station of forces. If we imagine a man deprived from his birth of all impressions, and by some miracle having preserved his life, such a man would not be capable of a single action or movement. In actual fact he could not live, as he could neither breathe nor feed. Life is a very complicated series of actions—breathing, feeding, interchange of matters, growth of cells and tissues, reflexes, nervous impulses and so on. A man lacking external impressions could not have any of these things, and of course he could not show those manifestations, those actions which are usually regarded as of the will and consciousness.

Thus from the positivist point of view man differs from animals only by the greater complexity of his reactions to external impressions, and by a longer interval between the impression and the reaction. But both man and animals lack independent actions, born within themselves, and what may be called will in man is nothing but the resultant of his wishes.

Such is a clearly positivist view. But there are very few who sincerely and consistently hold this view. Most men, while assuring themselves and others that they stand on the ground of a strictly scientific positivist world-concept, actually hold a mixture of theories, that is, they recognize the positivist view of things only to a certain degree, until it begins to be too austere and to offer too little consolation. Recognizing on the one hand that all physical and psychical processes in man are reflex in character, they admit at the same time some independent consciousness, some spiritual principle, and free will.

Will, from this point of view, is a certain combination derived from certain specially developed qualities, existing in a man capable of doing. Will is a sign of a being of a very high order of existence as compared with the being of an ordinary man. Only men who are in possession of such a being can do. All other men are merely automata, put into action by external forces like machines or clockwork toys, acting as much and as long as the wound-up spring within them acts, and not capable of adding anything to its force. Thus the teaching I am speaking about recognizes great possibilities in man, far greater than those which positive science sees, but denies to man as he is now any value as an entity of independence and will.

Man, such as we know him, is a machine. This idea of the mechanicalness of man must be very clearly understood and well-represented to oneself in order to see all its significance and all the consequences and results arising from it.

First of all everyone should understand his own mechanicalness. This understanding can come only as the result of a rightly formulated self-observation. As to self-observation—it is not so simple a thing as it may seem at first sight. Therefore the teaching puts as the foundation stone the study of the principles of right self-observation. But before passing to the study of these principles a man must make the decision that he will be absolutely sincere with himself, will not close his eyes to anything, will not turn aside from any results, wherever they may lead him, will not fear any deductions, will not limit himself to any previously erected walls. For a man unaccustomed to thinking in this direction, very much courage is required to accept sincerely the results and conclusions arrived at. They upset man's whole line of thinking and deprive him of his most pleasant and dearest illusions. He sees, first of all, his total impotence and helplessness in the face of literally everything that surrounds him. Everything possesses him, everything rules him. He does not possess, does not rule anything. Things attract or repel him. All his life is nothing but a blind following of those attractions and repulsions. Further, if he is not afraid of the conclusions, he sees how what he calls his character, tastes and habits are formed: in a word, how his personality and individuality are built up. But man's self-observation, however seriously and sincerely it may be carried out, by itself cannot draw for him an absolutely true picture of his internal mechanism.

The teaching which is being expounded gives general principles of the construction of the mechanism, and with the help of self-observation a man checks these principles. The first principle of this teaching is that nothing shall be taken on faith. The scheme of the construction of the human machine which he studies must serve a man only as a plan for his own work, in which the center of gravity lies.

Man is born, it is said, with a mechanism adapted for receiving many kinds of impressions. The perception of some of these impressions begins before birth; and during his growth more and more receiving apparatuses spring forth and become perfected.

The construction of these receiving apparatuses is the same, recalling the clean wax discs from which phonograph records are made. On these rolls and reels all the impressions received are noted down, from the first day of life and even before. Besides this, the mechanism has one more automatically acting adjustment, thanks to which all newly received impressions are connected with those previously recorded.

In addition to these a chronological record is kept. Thus every impression which has been experienced is written down in several places on several rolls. On these rolls it is preserved unchanged. What we call memory is a very imperfect adaptation by means of which we can keep on record only a small part of our store of impressions; but impressions once experienced never disappear; they are preserved on rolls where they are written down. Many experiences in hypnosis have been made and it has been stated with irrefutable examples that man remembers everything he has ever experienced down to the minutest detail. He remembers all the details of his surroundings, even the faces and voices of the people round him during his infancy, when he seemed to be an entirely unconscious being.

It is possible by hypnosis to make all the rolls turn, even to the deepest depths of the mechanism. But it may happen that these rolls begin to unroll by themselves as a result of some visible or hidden shock, and scenes, pictures or faces, apparently long forgotten, suddenly come to the surface. All the internal psychic life of man is nothing but an unfolding, before the mental vision, of these rolls with their records of impressions. All the peculiarities of a man's world conception and the characteristic features of his individuality depend on the order in which these records come and upon the quality of the rolls existing in him.

Let us suppose that some impression was experienced and recorded in connection with another having nothing in common with the first—for instance, some very bright dance tune has been heard by a man in a moment of intense psychic shock, distress or sorrow. Then this tune will always evoke in him the same negative emotion and correspondingly the feeling of distress will recall to him that bright dance tune. Science calls this associative thinking and feeling; but science does not realize how much man is bound by these associations and how he cannot get away from them. Man's world-conception is entirely defined by the character and quantity of these associations.

Now we see to a certain extent why men cannot understand each other when speaking about man. In order to speak about man in any serious manner it is necessary to know much, otherwise the conception of man becomes too entangled and too diffuse. Only when one knows the first principles of the human mechanism can one indicate which sides and which qualities one is going to speak about. A man who does not know will entangle both himself and his hearers. A conversation between several persons who speak about man without defining and indicating which man they are speaking about will never be a serious conversation but merely empty words without content. Consequently, in order to understand what man is, one must first understand what kinds of man may exist and in what ways they differ from one another. Meanwhile we must realize that we do not know.

Man is a plural being. When we speak of ourselves ordinarily, we speak of 'I.' We say, " 'I' did this," " 'I' think this," " 'I' want to do this"—but this is a mistake.

There is no such 'I,' or rather there are hundreds, thousands of little 'I's in every one of us. We are divided in ourselves but we cannot recognize the plurality of our being except by observation and study. At one moment it is one 'I' that acts, at the next moment it is another 'I.' It is because the 'I's' in ourselves are contradictory that we do not function harmoniously.

We live ordinarily with only a very minute part of our functions and our strength, because we do not recognize that we are machines, and we do not know the nature and working of our mechanism. We are machines.

We are governed entirely by external circumstances. All our actions follow the line of least resistance to the pressure of outside circumstances.

Try for yourselves: can you govern your emotions? No. You may try to suppress them or cast out one emotion by another emotion. But you cannot control it. It controls you. Or you may decide to do something—your intellectual 'I' may make such a decision. But when the time comes to do it, you may find yourself doing just the opposite.

If circumstances are favorable to your decision you may do it, but if they are unfavorable you will do whatever they direct. You do not control your actions. You are a machine and external circumstances govern your actions irrespective of your desires.

I do not say nobody can control his actions. I say you can't, because you are divided. There are two parts to you, a strong and a weak part. If your strength grows, your weakness will also grow, and will become negative strength unless you learn to stop it.

If we learn to control our actions, that will be different. When a certain level of being is reached we can really control every part of ourself—but, as we are now, we cannot even do what we decide to do.

(*Here a theosophist posed a question claiming that we could change conditions.*)

Answer: Conditions never change—they are always the same. There is no change, only modification of circumstances.

Question: Isn't it a change if a man becomes better?

Answer: One man means nothing to humanity. One man becomes better, another becomes worse—it is always the same.

Question: But is it not an improvement for a liar to become truthful?

Answer: No, it is the same thing. First he tells lies mechanically because he cannot tell the truth; then he will tell the truth mechanically because it is now easier for him. Truth and lies are only valuable in relation to ourselves if we can control them. Such as we are we cannot be moral because we are mechanical. Morality is relative—subjective, contradictory and mechanical. It is the same with us: physical man, emotional man, intellectual man—each has a different set of morals befitting his nature. The machine in every man is divided into three basic parts, three centers.

Look at yourself at any moment and ask: "What sort of 'I' is it that is working at the moment? Does it belong to my intellectual center, to my emotional center or to my moving center?"

You will probably find that it is quite different from what you imagine, but it will be one of these.

Question: Is there no absolute code of morality that ought to be binding on all men alike?

Answer: Yes. When we can use all the forces that control our centers—then we can be moral. But until then, as long as we use only a part of our functions, we cannot be moral. We act mechanically in all that we do, and machines cannot be moral.

Question: It seems a hopeless position?

Answer: Quite right. It is hopeless.

Question: Then how can we change ourselves, and use all our forces?

Answer: That is another matter. The chief cause of our weakness is our inability to apply our will to all three of our centers simultaneously.

Question: Can we apply our will to any of them?

Answer: Certainly, sometimes we do. Sometimes we may even be able to control one of them for a moment with very extraordinary results. (*He relates the story of a prisoner throwing a ball of paper with a message to his wife through a high and difficult window.*) This is his only means to become

free. If he fails the first time he will never have another
chance. He succeeds for the moment in having absolute control over his physical center so that he is able to accomplish
what otherwise he never could have done.

Question: Do you know anybody who has reached this
higher plane of being?

Answer: It means nothing if I say yes or no. If I say yes, you
cannot verify it and if I say no, you are none the wiser. You
have no business to believe me. I ask you to believe nothing
that you cannot verify for yourself.

Question: If we are wholly mechanical, how are we to get
control over ourselves? Can a machine control itself?

Answer: Quite right—of course not. We cannot change ourselves. We can only modify ourselves a little. But we can be
changed with help from the outside.

The theory of esotericism is that mankind consists of two
circles: a large, outer circle, embracing all human beings, and
a small circle of instructed and understanding people at the
center. Real instruction, which alone can change us, can only
come from this center, and the aim of this teaching is to help
us to prepare ourselves to receive such instruction.

By ourselves we cannot change ourselves—that can come
only from outside.

Every religion points to the existence of a common center of
knowledge. In every sacred book knowledge is there, but people do not wish to know it.

Question: But haven't we a great store of knowledge already?

Answer: Yes, too many kinds of knowledge. Our present
knowledge is based on sense perceptions—like children's. If we

wish to acquire the right kind of knowledge, we must change ourselves. With a development of our being we can find a higher state of consciousness. Change of knowledge comes from change of being. Knowledge in itself is nothing. We must first have self-knowledge, and with the help of self-knowledge, we shall learn how to change ourselves—if we wish to change ourselves.

Question: And this change must still come from without?

Answer: Yes. When we are ready for new knowledge it will come to us.

Question: Can one alter one's emotions by acts of judgment?

Answer: One center of our machine cannot change another center. For example: in London I am irritable, the weather and the climate dispirit me and make me bad-tempered, whereas in India I am good-tempered. Therefore my judgment tells me to go to India and I shall drive out the emotion of irritability. But then, in London, I find I can work; in the tropics not as well. And so, there I should be irritable for another reason. You see, emotions exist independently of the judgment and you cannot alter one by means of the other.

Question: What is a higher state of being?

Answer: There are several states of consciousness:
1) sleep, in which our machine still functions but at very low pressure.
2) waking state, as we are at this moment.
These two are all that the average man knows.
3) what is called self-consciousness. It is the moment when a man is aware both of himself and of his machine. We have it in flashes, but only in flashes. There are moments when you become aware not only of what you are doing but also of your-

self doing it. You see both 'I' and the 'here' of 'I am here'—both the anger and the 'I' that is angry. Call this self-remembering, if you like.

Now when you are fully and always aware of the 'I' and what it is doing and which 'I' it is—you become conscious of yourself. Self-consciousness is the third state.

Question: Is it not easier when one is passive?

Answer: Yes, but useless. You must observe the machine when it is working. There are states beyond the third state of consciousness, but there is no need to speak of them now. Only a man in the highest state of being is a complete man. All the others are merely fractions of man. The outside help which is necessary will come from teachers or from the teaching I am following. The starting points of this self-observation are:

1) that we are not one.

2) that we have no control over ourselves. We do not control our own mechanism.

3) we do not remember ourselves. If I say 'I am reading a book' and do not know that 'I' am reading, that is one thing, but when I am conscious that 'I' am reading, that is self-remembering.

Question: Doesn't cynicism result?

Answer: Quite true. If you go no further than to see that you and all men are machines, you will simply become cynical. But if you carry your work on, you will cease to be cynical.

Question: Why?

Answer: Because you will have to make a choice, to decide —to seek either to become completely mechanical or completely conscious. This is the parting of the ways of which all mystical teachings speak.

Question: Are there no other ways of doing what I want to do?

Answer: In England, no. In the East, it is different. There are different methods for different men. But you must find a teacher. You alone can decide what it is that you wish to do. Search into your heart for what you most desire and if you are capable of doing it, you will know what to do.

Think well about it, and then go forward.

One-sided development

In each of those present here one of his inner machines is more developed than the others. There is no connection between them. Only he can be called a man without quotation marks in whom all three machines are developed. A one-sided development is only harmful. If a man possesses knowledge and even knows all he must do, this knowledge is useless and can even do harm. All of you are deformed. If only personality is developed it is deformity; such a man can in no way be called a complete man—he is a quarter, a third of a man. The same applies to a man with a developed essence or a man with developed muscles. Nor can he be called a complete man in whom a more or less developed personality is combined with a developed body, while his essence remains totally undeveloped. In short, a man in whom only two of the three machines are developed cannot be called a man. A man of such one-sided development has more desires in a given sphere, desires he cannot satisfy and at the same time cannot renounce. Life becomes miserable for him. For this state of fruitless, half-satisfied desires I can find no more suitable word than onanism. From the standpoint of the ideal of full harmonious development such a one-sided man is worthless.

The reception of external impressions depends on the

rhythm of the external stimulators of impressions 'and on the rhythm of the senses. Right reception of impressions is possible only if these rhythms correspond to one another. If I or anyone were to say two words, one of them would be said with one understanding, another with another. Each of my words has a definite rhythm. If I say twelve words, in each of my listeners some words—say three—would be taken in by the body, seven by personality and two by essence. Since the machines are not connected with each other, each part of the listener has recorded only part of what was said; in recollecting, the general impression is lost and cannot be reproduced. The same happens when a man wants to express something to another. Owing to the absence of connection between the machines he is able to express only a fraction of himself.

Every man wants something, but first he must find out and verify all that is wrong or lacking in himself, and he must bear in mind that a man can never be a man if he has no right rhythms in himself.

Take the reception of sound. A sound reaches the receiving apparatuses of all the three machines simultaneously but owing to the fact that the rhythms of the machines are different, only one of them has time to receive the impression, for the receiving faculty of the others lags behind. If a man hears the sound with his thinking faculty and is too slow to pass it on to the body, for which it is destined, then the next sound he hears, also destined for the body, drives away the first completely and the required result is not obtained. If a man decides to do something, for instance to hit something or someone, and at the moment of decision the body does not fulfill this decision since it was not quick enough to receive it in time, the force of the blow will be much weaker or there will be no blow at all.

Just as in the case of reception, a man's manifestations, too, can never be complete. Sorrow, joy, hunger, cold, envy and other feelings and sensations are experienced only by a part of an ordinary man's being, instead of by the whole of him.

Question: What is the method of the Institute?

Answer: The method is a subjective one, that is, it depends on the individual peculiarities of each person. There is only one general rule which can be applied to everyone—observation. This is indispensable for all. However, this observation is not for change but for seeing oneself. Everyone has his own peculiarities, his own habits which a man usually does not see. One must see those peculiarities. In this way one may "discover many Americas." Every small fact has its own basic cause. When you have collected material about yourselves it will be possible to speak; at present, conversation is only theoretical.

If we put weight on one side, we must balance it in some way. By trying to observe ourselves, we get practice in concentration, which will be useful even in ordinary life.

Question: What is the role of suffering in self-development?

Answer: There are two kinds of suffering—conscious and unconscious. Only a fool suffers unconsciously.

[84]

In life there are two rivers, two directions. In the first, the law is for the river itself, not for the drops of water. We are drops. At one moment a drop is at the surface, at another moment at the bottom. Suffering depends on its position. In the first river, suffering is completely useless because it is accidental and unconscious.

Parallel with this river is another river. In this other river there is a different kind of suffering. The drop in the first river has the possibility of passing into the second. Today the drop suffers because yesterday it did not suffer enough. Here the law of retribution operates. The drop can also suffer in advance. Sooner or later everything is paid for. For the Cosmos there is no time. Suffering can be voluntary and only voluntary suffering has value. One may suffer simply because one feels unhappy. Or one may suffer for yesterday and to prepare for tomorrow.

I repeat, only voluntary suffering has value.

Question: Was Christ a teacher with a school preparation, or was he an accidental genius?

Answer: Without knowledge he could not have been what he was, nor could he have done what he did. It is known that where he was there was knowledge.

Question: If we are only mechanical, what sense has religion?

Answer: For some, religion is a law, a guidance, a direction; for others—a policeman.

Question: In what sense was it said in an earlier lecture that the earth is alive?

Answer: It is not only we who are alive. If a part is alive, then the whole is alive. The whole universe is like a chain, and the earth is one link in this chain. Where there is movement, there is life.

Question: In what sense was it said that one who has not died cannot be born?

Answer: All religions speak about death during this life on earth. Death must come before rebirth. But what must die? False confidence in one's own knowledge, self-love and egoism. Our egoism must be broken. We must realize that we are very complicated machines, and so this process of breaking is bound to be a long and difficult task. Before real growth becomes possible, our personality must die.

Question: Did Christ teach dances?

Answer: I was not there to see. It is necessary to distinguish between dances and gymnastics—they are different things. We do not know whether his disciples danced, but we do know that where Christ got his training they certainly taught "sacred gymnastics."

Question: Is there any value in Catholic ceremonies and rites?

Answer: I have not studied Catholic ritual, but I know the rituals of the Greek Church well, and there, underlying the form and ceremony, there is real meaning. Every ceremony, if it continues to be practiced without change, has value. Ritual is like ancient dances which were guidebooks where truth was written down. But to understand one must have a key.

Old country dances also have meaning—some even contain such things as recipes for making jam.

A ceremony is a book in which much is written. Anyone who understands can read it. In one ceremony more is contained than in a hundred books. Usually everything changes, but customs and ceremonies can remain unchanged.

Question: Does reincarnation of souls exist?

Answer: A soul is a luxury. No one has yet been born with a fully developed soul. Before we can speak of reincarnation, we must know what kind of man we are speaking about, what kind of soul and what kind of reincarnation. A soul may disintegrate immediately after death, or it may do so after a certain time. For example, a soul may be crystallized within the limits of the earth and may remain there, yet not be crystallized for the sun.

Question: Can women work as well as men?

Answer: Different parts are more highly developed in men and women. In men it is the intellectual part, which we will call A; in women the emotional, or B. Work in the Institute is sometimes more along the lines of A, in which case it is very difficult for B. At other times it is more along the lines of B, in which case it is harder for A. But what is essential for real understanding is the fusion of A and B. This produces a force that we shall call C.

Yes, there are equal chances for men and for women.

Self-observation is very difficult. The more you try, the more clearly you will see this.

At present you should practice it not for results but to understand that you cannot observe yourselves. In the past you imagined that you saw and knew yourselves.

I am speaking of objective self-observation. Objectively you cannot see yourselves for a single minute, because it is a different function, the function of the master.

If it seems to you that you can observe yourselves for five minutes, this is wrong; if it is for twenty minutes or for one minute—it is equally wrong. If you simply realize that you cannot, it will be right. To come to it is your aim.

To achieve this aim, you must try and try.

When you try, the result will not be, in the true sense, self-observation. But trying will strengthen your attention, you will learn to concentrate better. All this will be useful later. Only then can one begin to remember oneself.

If you work conscientiously, you will remember yourselves not more but less, because self-remembering requires many things. It is not so easy, it costs a great deal.

The exercise of self-observation is sufficient for several

years. Do not attempt anything else. If you work conscientiously, you will see what you need.

At present you have but one attention, either in the body or the feeling.

Question: How can we gain attention?

Answer: There is no attention in people. You must aim to acquire this. Self-observation is only possible after acquiring attention. Start on small things.

Question: What small things can we start on? What should we do?

Answer: Your nervous and restless movements make everyone know, consciously or unconsciously, that you have no authority and are a booby. With these restless movements you cannot be anything. The first thing for you to do is to stop these movements. Make this your aim, your God. Even get your family to help you. Only after this, you can perhaps gain attention. This is an example of doing.

Another example—an aspiring pianist can never learn except little by little. If you wish to play melodies without first practicing, you can never play real melodies. The melodies you will play will be cacophonous and will make people suffer and hate you. It is the same with psychological ideas: to gain anything, long practice is necessary.

Try to accomplish very small things first. If at first you aim at big things you will never be anything. And your manifestations will act like cacophonous melodies and cause people to hate you.

Question: What must I do?

Answer: There are two kinds of doing—automatic doing, and doing according to aim. Take a small thing which you now are not able to do, and make this your aim, your God. Let nothing interfere. Only aim at this. Then, if you succeed in doing this, I will be able to give you a greater task. Now you have an appetite to do things too big for you. This is an abnormal appetite. You can never do these things, and this appetite keeps you from doing the small things you might do. Destroy this appetite, forget big things. Make the breaking of a small habit your aim.

Question: I think my worst fault is talking too much. Would trying not to talk so much be a good task?

Answer: For you this is a very good aim. You spoil everything with your talking. This talk even hinders your business. When you talk much, your words have no weight. Try to overcome this. Many blessings will flow to you if you succeed. Truly, this is a very good task. But it is a big thing, not small. I promise you, if you achieve this, even if I am not here, I will know about your achievement, and will send help so that you will know what to do next.

Question: Would a good task be to endure the manifestations of others?

Answer: To endure the manifestations of others is a big thing. The last thing for a man. Only a perfect man can do this. Start by making your aim or your God the ability to bear one manifestation of one person that you cannot now endure without nervousness. If you "wish," you "can." Without "wishing," you never "can." Wish is the most powerful thing in the world. With conscious wish everything comes.

Question: I frequently remember my aim but I have not the energy to do what I feel I should do.

Answer: Man has no energy to fulfill voluntary aims because all his strength, acquired at night during his passive state, is used up in negative manifestations. These are his automatic manifestations, the opposite of his positive, willed manifestations.

For those of you who are already able to remember your aim automatically, but have no strength to do it: Sit for a period of at least one hour alone. Make all your muscles relaxed. Allow your associations to proceed but do not be absorbed by them. Say to them: "If you will let me do as I wish now, I shall later grant you your wishes." Look on your associations as though they belonged to someone else, to keep yourself from identifying with them.

At the end of an hour take a piece of paper and write your aim on it. Make this paper your God. Everything else is nothing. Take it out of your pocket and read it constantly, every day. In this way it becomes part of you, at first theoretically, later actually. To gain energy, practice this exercise of sitting still and making your muscles dead. Only when everything in you is quiet after an hour, make your decision about your aim. Don't let associations absorb you. To undertake a voluntary aim, and to achieve it, gives magnetism and the ability to "do."

Question: What is magnetism?

Answer: Man has two substances in him, the substance of active elements of the physical body, and the substance made up of the active elements of astral matter. These two form a third substance by mixing. This mixed substance gathers in certain parts of a man and also forms an atmosphere around him, like the atmosphere surrounding a planet. Planetary atmospheres are continually gaining or losing substances because of other planets. Man is surrounded by other men, just as planets are surrounded by other planets. Within certain limits, when two atmospheres meet, and if the atmospheres are "sympathetic," a connection is made between them and lawful results occur. Something flows. The amount of atmosphere remains the same, but the quality changes. Man can control his atmosphere. It is like electricity, having positive and negative parts. One part can be increased and made to flow like a current. Everything has positive and negative electricity. In man, wishes and non-wishes may be positive and negative. Astral material always opposes physical material.

In ancient times priests were able to cure disease by blessing. Some priests had to lay their hands on the sick person. Some could cure at a short distance, some at a great distance. A "priest" was a man who had mixed substances and could cure others. A priest was a magnetizer. Sick persons have not enough mixed substances, not enough magnetism, not enough "life." This "mixed substance" can be seen if it is concentrated. An aura or halo was a real thing and can sometimes be seen at holy places or in churches. Mesmer rediscovered the use of this substance.

To be able to use this substance, you must first acquire it. It is the same with attention. It is gained only through conscious labor and intentional suffering, through doing small things voluntarily. Make some small aim your God, and you will be going toward acquiring magetism. Like electricity, magnetism can be concentrated and made to flow. In a real group, a real answer could be given to this question.

Everyone is in great need of one particular exercise, both if one wants to continue working and for external life.

We have two lives, inner and outer life, and so we also have two kinds of considering. We constantly consider.

When she looks at me, I feel inside a dislike of her, I am cross with her, but externally I am polite because I must be very polite since I need her. Internally I am what I am, but externally I am different. This is external considering. Now she says that I am a fool. This angers me. The fact that I am angered is the result, but what takes place in me is internal considering.

This internal and external considering are different. We must learn to be able to control separately both kinds of considering: the internal and the external. We want to change not only inside but also outside.

Yesterday, when she gave me an unfriendly look, I was cross. But today I understand that perhaps the reason why she looked at me like that is that she is a fool; or perhaps she had learned or heard something about me. And today I want to remain calm. She is a slave and I should not be angry with her inwardly. From today onward I want to be calm inside.

Outwardly I want today to be polite, but if necessary I can

appear angry. Outwardly it must be what is best for her and for me. I must consider. Internal and external considering must be different. In an ordinary man the external attitude is the result of the internal. If she is polite, I am also polite. But these attitudes should be separated.

Internally one should be free from considering, but externally one should do more than one has been doing so far. An ordinary man lives as he is dictated to from inside.

When we speak of change, we presume the need of inner change. Externally if everything is all right, there is no need to change. If it is not all right, perhaps there is no need to change either, because maybe it is original. What is necessary is to change inside.

Until now we did not change anything, but from today we want to change. But how to change? First, we must separate and then sort out, discard what is useless and build something new. Man has much that is good and much that is bad. If we discard everything, later it will be necessary to collect again.

If a man has not enough on the external side, he will need to fill the gaps. Who is not well educated should be better educated. But this is for life.

The work needs nothing external. Only the internal is needed. Externally, one should play a role in everything. Externally a man should be an actor, otherwise he does not answer the requirements of life. One man likes one thing; another, another thing: if you want to be a friend to both and behave in one way, one of them will not like it; if you behave in another way, the other will not like it. You should behave with one as he likes it and with the other as this other likes it. Then your life will be easier.

But inside it must be different: different in relation to the one and the other.

As things are now, especially in our times, every man considers utterly mechanically. We react to everything affecting us from outside. Now we obey orders. She is good, and I am good; she is bad, and I am bad. I am as she wants me to be, I am a puppet. But she too is a mechanical puppet. She also obeys orders mechanically and does what another one wants.

We must cease reacting inside. If someone is rude, we must not react inside. Whoever manages to do this will be more free. It is very difficult.

Inside us we have a horse; it obeys orders from outside. And our mind is too weak to do anything inside. Even if the mind gives the order to stop, nothing will stop inside.

We educate nothing but our mind. We know how to behave with such and such. "Goodbye." "How do you do?" But it is only the driver who knows this. Sitting on his box he has read about it. But the horse has no education whatever. It has not even been taught the alphabet, it knows no languages, it never went to school. The horse was also capable of being taught, but we forgot all about it. . . . And so it grew up a neglected orphan. It only knows two words: right and left.

What I said about inner change refers only to the need of change in the horse. If the horse changes, we can change even externally. If the horse does not change, everything will remain the same, no matter how long we study.

It is easy to decide to change sitting quietly in your room. But as soon as you meet someone, the horse kicks. Inside us we have a horse.

The horse must change.

If anyone thinks that self-study will help and he will be able to change, he is greatly mistaken. Even if he reads all the books, studies for a hundred years, masters all knowledge, all mysteries—nothing will come of it.

Because all this knowledge will belong to the driver. And he, even if he knows, cannot drag the cart without the horse—it is too heavy.

First of all you must realize that you are not you. Be sure of that, believe me. You are the horse, and if you wish to start working, the horse must be taught a language in which you can talk to it, tell it what you know and prove to it the necessity of, say, changing its disposition. If you succeed in this, then, with your help, the horse too will begin to learn.

But change is possible only inside.

As to the cart, its existence was completely forgotten. Yet it is also a part, and an important part, of the team. It has its own life, which is the basis of our life. It has its own psychology. It also thinks, is hungry, has desires, takes part in the common work. It too should have been educated, sent to school, but neither the parents nor anyone else cared. Only the driver was taught. He knows languages, knows where such and such a street is. But he cannot drive there alone.

Originally our cart was built for an ordinary town; all the mechanical parts were designed to suit the road. The cart has many small wheels. The idea was that the unevennesses of the road would distribute the lubricating oil evenly and thus oil them. But all this was calculated for a certain town where the roads are not too smooth. Now the town has changed, but the make of the cart has remained the same. It was made to cart luggage, but now it carries passengers. And it always drives along one and the same street, the "Broadway." Some parts got rusty from long disuse. If, at times, it needs to drive along a different street, it seldom escapes a breakdown and a more or less serious overhaul afterwards. Badly or well, it can still work on the "Broadway," but for another street it must first be altered.

Every cart has its own momentum, but in certain senses our cart has lost it. And it cannot work without momentum.

Moreover the horse can pull, say, only fifty kilos, whereas the cart can take a hundred kilos. So even if they wish to, they cannot work together.

Some machines are so damaged that nothing can be done with them. They can only be sold. Others can still be mended. But this requires a long time, for some of the parts are too damaged. The machine has to be taken to pieces, all the metal parts have to be put in oil, cleaned and then put together again. Some of them will have to be replaced. Certain parts are cheap and can be bought, but others are expensive and cannot be replaced—the cost would be too high. Sometimes it is cheaper to buy a new car than to repair an old one.

Quite possibly all those who sit here wish and can wish only with one part of themselves. Again it is only with the driver, for he has read something, heard something. He has many fantasies, he even flies to the moon in his dreams.

Those who think that they can do something with themselves are greatly mistaken. To change something within is very difficult. What you know, it is the driver who knows it. All your knowledge is just manipulations. Real change is a very difficult thing, more difficult than finding several hundred thousand dollars in the street.

Question: Why was the horse not educated?

Answer: The grandfather and grandmother gradually forgot, and all the relatives forgot. Education needs time, needs suffering; life becomes less peaceful. At first they did not educate it through laziness, and later they forgot altogether.

Here again, the law of three works. Between the positive and the negative principles there must be friction, suffering. Suffering leads to the third principle. It is a hundred times easier to be passive so that suffering and result happen outside and not inside you. Inner result is achieved when everything takes place inside you.

Sometimes we are active, at other times we are passive. For one hour we are active, for another hour passive.

When we are active we are being spent, when we are passive we rest. But when everything is inside you, you cannot rest, the law acts always. Even if you do not suffer, you are not quiet.

Every man dislikes suffering, every man wants to be quiet. Every man chooses what is easiest, least disturbing, tries not to think too much. Little by little our grandfather and grandmother rested more and more. The first day, five minutes of rest; the next day, ten minutes; and so on. A moment came when half of the time was spent on rest. And the law is such that if one thing increases by a unit, another thing decreases by a unit. Where there is more it is added, where there is less it is reduced. Gradually your grandfather and grandmother forgot about educating the horse. And now no one remembers any more.

Question: How to begin inner change?

Answer: My advice—what I said about considering. You should begin to teach the horse a new language, prepare it for the desire to change.

The cart and the horse are connected. The horse and the driver are also connected by the reins. The horse knows two words—right and left. At times the driver cannot give orders to the horse because our reins have the capacity now to thicken, now to become more thin. They are not made of leather. When our reins become more thin, the driver cannot control the horse. The horse knows only the language of the reins. No matter how much the driver shouts, "Please, right," the horse does not budge. If he pulls, it understands. Perhaps the horse knows some language, but not the one the driver knows. Maybe it is Arabic.

The same situation exists between the horse and the cart, with the shafts. This requires another explanation.

We have something like magnetism in us. It consists not only of one substance but of several. It is an important part of us. It is formed when the machine is working.

When we spoke about food we spoke of only one octave. But there are three octaves there. One octave produces one substance, the others produce different substances. Si is the result of the first octave. When the machine works mechanically, substance No. 1 is produced. When we work subconsciously, another kind of substance is produced. If there is no subconscious work of this kind, this substance is not produced. When we work consciously, a third kind of substance is produced.

Let us examine these three. The first corresponds to the shafts, the second to the reins, the third to the substance which permits the driver to hear the passenger. You know that sound cannot travel in vacuum, there must be some substance there.

We must understand the difference between a casual passenger and the master of the cart. "I" is the master, if we have an "I." If we have not, there is always someone sitting in the cart and giving orders to the driver. Between the passenger and the driver there is a substance which allows the driver to hear. Whether these substances are there or not depends on many accidental things. It may be absent. If the substance has accumulated, the passenger can give orders to the driver, but the driver cannot order the horse, and so on. At times you can, at others you cannot, it depends on the amount of substance there is. Tomorrow you can, today you cannot. This substance is the result of many things.

One of these substances is formed when we suffer. We suffer whenever we are not mechanically quiet. There are different kinds of suffering. For instance, I want to tell you something, but I feel it is best to say nothing. One side wants to tell, the other wants to keep silent. The struggle produces a substance. Gradually this substance collects in a certain place.

Question: What is inspiration?

Answer: Inspiration is an association. It is the work of one center. Inspiration is cheap, rest assured of that. Only conflict, argument, may produce a result.

Whenever there is an active element there is a passive element. If you believe in God, you also believe in the devil. All this has no value. Whether you are good or bad—it is not worth anything. Only a conflict between two sides is worth something. Only when much is accumulated can something new manifest itself.

At every moment there may be a conflict in you. You never see yourself. You will believe what I say only when you begin to look into yourself—then you will see. If you try to do something you don't want to do—you will suffer. If you want to do something and don't do it—you also suffer.

What you like—whether good or bad—is of the same value. Good is a relative concept. Only if you begin to work, your good and bad begin to exist.

Question: Conflict of two desires leads to suffering. Yet some suffering leads to a madhouse.

Answer: Suffering can be of different kinds. To begin with, we shall divide it into two kinds. First, unconscious; second, conscious.

The first kind bears no results. For instance, you suffer from hunger because you have no money to buy bread. If you have some bread and don't eat it and suffer, it is better.

If you suffer with one center, either thinking or feeling, you get to a lunatic asylum.

Suffering must be harmonious. There must be correspondence between the fine and the coarse. Otherwise something may break.

You have many centers: not three, not five, not six, but more. Between them there is a place where argument may take place. But equilibrium may be upset. You have built a house, but the equilibrium is upset, the house falls down and everything is spoiled.

Now I am explaining things theoretically in order to provide material for mutual understanding.

To do something, however small, is a great risk. Suffering may have a serious result. I now speak about suffering theoretically, for understanding. But it is only now I do so. At the Institute they do not think about future life, they only think about tomorrow. Man cannot see and cannot believe. Only when he knows himself, knows his inner structure, only then can he see. Now we study in an external manner.

It is possible to study the sun, the moon. But man has everything within him. I have inside me the sun, the moon, God. I am—all life in its totality.

To understand one must know oneself.

PRIEURÉ, JANUARY 17, 1923

Every animal works according to its constitution. One animal works more, another less, but all work each as much as is natural to it. We also work; among us, one is more capable for work, another less. Whoever works like an ox is worthless and whoever does not work is also worthless. The value of work is not in quantity but in quality. Unfortunately I must say that all our people do not work too well as regards quality. However, let the work which they have done so far serve as a source of remorse. If it will serve as a cause for remorse, it will be of use; if not, it is good for nothing.

Every animal, as already said, works according to what animal it is. One animal—say, a worm—works quite mechanically; one cannot expect anything else from it. It has no other brain but a mechanical one. Another animal works and moves solely by feeling—such is the structure of its brain. A third animal perceives movement, which is called work, only through intellect, and one cannot demand from it anything else as it has no other brain; nothing else can be expected as nature created it with this kind of brain.

Thus the quality of work depends on what brain there is. When we consider different kinds of animals, we find that there are one-brained, two-brained and three-brained animals.

[103]

Man is a three-brained animal. But it often happens that he who has three brains must work, say, five times more than he who has two brains. Man is so created that more work is demanded from him than he can produce according to his constitution. It is not man's fault, but the fault of nature. Work will be of value only when man gives as much as is the limit of possibility. Normally in man's work the participation of feeling and thought is necessary. If one of these functions is absent, the quality of the man's work will be on the level of work done by one who works with two brains. If man wants to work like a man he must learn to work like a man. This is easy to determine—just as easy as to distinguish between animal and man—and we shall soon learn to see it. Until then, you have to take my word for it. All you need is to discriminate with your mind.

I say that until now you have not been working like men; but there is a possibility to learn to work like men. Working like a man means that a man feels what he is doing and thinks why and for what he does it, how he is doing it now, how it had to be done yesterday and how today, how he would have to do it tomorrow, and how it is generally best to get it done —whether there is a better way. If man works rightly, he will succeed in doing better and better work. But when a two-brained creature works, there is no difference between its work yesterday, today or tomorrow.

During our work, not a single man worked like a man. But for the Institute it is essential to work differently. Each must work for himself, for others can do nothing for him. If you can make, say, a cigarette like a man, you already know how to make a carpet. All the necessary apparatus is given to man for doing everything. Every man can do whatever others can do. If one man can, everyone can. Genius, talent, is all nonsense. The secret is simple, to do things like a man. Who can think and do things like a man can at once do a thing as well as another who has been doing it all his life but not like a man. What had to be learned by this one in ten years, the other learns in two

or three days and he then does it better than the one who
spent his life doing it. I have met people who, before learning,
worked all their lives not like men, but when they had
learned, they could easily do the finest work as well as the
roughest, work they had never even seen before. The secret is
small and very easy—one must learn to work like a man. And
that is when a man does a thing and at the same time he
thinks about what he is doing and studies how the work
should be done, and while doing it forgets all—his grandmother and grandfather and his dinner.

In the beginning it is very difficult. I will give you theoretical indications as to how to work, the rest will depend on each
individual man. But I warn you that I shall say only as much
as you put into practice. The more there is put into practice,
the more I shall say. Even if people do so only for an hour, I
shall talk to them as long as is necessary, twenty-four hours if
need be. But to those who will continue to work as before—to
the devil!

As I said, the essence of correct man's work is in the working together of the three centers—moving, emotional and
thinking. When all three work together and produce an action,
this is the work of a man. There is a thousand times more
value even in polishing the floor as it should be done than in
writing twenty-five books. But before starting to work with all
centers and concentrating them on the work, it is necessary to
prepare each center separately so that each could concentrate.
It is necessary to train the moving center to work with the others. And one must remember that each center consists of three.

Our moving center is more or less adapted.

The second center, as difficulties go, is the thinking center
and the most difficult, the emotional. We already begin to succeed in small things with our moving center. But neither the
thinking nor the emotional center can concentrate at all. To
succeed in collecting thoughts in a desired direction is not
what is wanted. When we succeed in this, it is mechanical

concentration which everybody can have—it is not the concentration of a man. It is important to know how not to depend on associations, and we shall therefore begin with the thinking center. We shall exercise the moving center by continuing the same exercises we have done so far.

Before going any further, it would be useful to learn to think according to a definite order. Let everyone take some object. Let each of you ask himself questions relating to the object and answer these according to his knowledge and material:

1) Its origin
2) The cause of its origin
3) Its history
4) Its qualities and attributes
5) Objects connected with it and related to it
6) Its use and application
7) Its results and effects
8) What it explains and proves
9) Its end or its future
10) Your opinion, the cause and motives of this opinion.

For one section of the people here, their stay has become completely useless. If th: section were asked why they are here, they would either be completely unable to answer or they would answer something quite nonsensical, would produce a whole philosophy, themselves not believing what they were saying. A few may have known at the beginning why they came, but they have forgotten. I take it that everyone who comes here has realized the necessity of doing something, that he has already tried by himself, and that his attempts have led him to the conclusion that in the conditions of ordinary life it is impossible to achieve anything. And so he begins to make inquiries, to search for places where, owing to prearranged conditions, work on oneself is possible. At last he finds; he learns that here such work is possible. And indeed such a place has been created here and organized so that the seeker should be in the conditions he was looking for.

But the section of people I am speaking about does not make use of these conditions; I may even say they do not see these conditions. And the fact that they do not see them proves that in reality these people were not looking for them, and have not tried in their everyday life to get what they were supposed to be looking for. Whoever does not make use of the

conditions here for work on himself and does not see them—
this is no place for him. He is wasting his time by remaining
here, hindering others and taking someone else's place. Our
space is limited and there are many applicants whom I have to
refuse for lack of space. You must either make use of this place
or go away and not waste your time and take someone else's
place.

I repeat, I start from the point that presumably those who
come here have already done preparatory work, have been to
lectures, have made attempts to work by themselves, and so
on.

As I see it, those who are here have already realized the necessity of work on themselves and almost know how it should
be done, but are unable, for reasons which are beyond their
control. In consequence there is no need to repeat again why
each of you is here.

I can carry on my work here only if what has already been
received is transmuted into practical life. Unfortunately nothing of the sort takes place, because people live here but do not
work; they do so only under coercion, outwardly, like day la-
borers in ordinary life. I therefore propose to this section of
people that they should work now as they once understood
work, that they should reawaken the ideas they once had, and
set to work in earnest, or that they should understand at once
that their presence here is useless. As things are now, if they
go on for ten years nothing will result.

I am not answerable for anything. Let people try. Otherwise
they may present a claim for the time wasted. Let them arouse
in themselves their former intentions and so make their stay
here useful for themselves and for those around them.

He who can be a conscious egoist here can be not an egoist
in life. To be an egoist here means not to give a hoot for anyone, myself included; to regard everyone and everything as
something by which to help oneself. There must be no considering with anything or with anyone. Who is mad, who is
clever does not matter. A madman is also a good subject for

study, for work. And so is a clever man. In other words, both mad and clever people are necessary. Both the cad and the decent man are needed; for the fool and the clever man, the cad and the decent man can equally serve as a mirror and a shock for seeing, studying and using for work on oneself.

Moreover, you should understand for your own guidance one particular phenomenon.

Our Institute is like the repair shop of a railroad, or like a garage where repairs are carried out. When an engine or a car is in the shop, and a new man comes into the shop, he sees engines which he has never seen before. And, indeed, all the cars he sees outside are covered over and painted, and the man in the street has never seen their insides. The eyes of the man in the street are only used to seeing the covering. He does not see them without the covering as in the repair shop, where parts are dismantled and all stand cleaned and open to view, having nothing in common with the appearance familiar to the eye. And so it is here. When a new person arrives with his luggage, he is at once undressed. And then all his worst sides, all his inner "beauties" become evident.

This is why those among you who do not know about this phenomenon get the impression that we have indeed collected here only people who are stupid, lazy, dense—in a word, all riff-raff. But they forget one important thing; that it is not he who discovers this, but that someone has exposed them. But he sees and ascribes everything to himself. If he is a fool, he does not see that he himself is a fool and does not realize that someone else has exposed others. If someone else had not exposed them perhaps he would have been bending the knee to one of these fools. He sees him undressed, but forgets that he too is undressed. He imagines that just as in life he could wear a mask, so here too he can put on a mask. But directly he entered these gates, the watchman took off his mask. Here he is naked, everybody senses directly what sort of person he is. That is why no one must consider internally with anybody here. If a person has done wrong, do not be indignant, because you too have done the same. On the contrary, you should be very thankful and think yourself lucky that you did not get a slap in the face from anyone, for at every step you act wrongly toward someone else. Therefore how kind these people must be who do not consider with you. Whereas, if someone has done you the slightest wrong, you already want to hit him in the face.

You must understand this clearly and behave accordingly and try to make use of other people in all their aspects, good and bad; and you must also help others in all your own aspects, whatever they may be. Whether the other man is clever, a fool, kind, despicable, be assured that at different times you also are stupid and clever, despicable and conscientious. All people are the same, only they manifest themselves differently at different times, just as you yourself are different at different times. Just as you need help at different times, so others need your help, but you must help others not for their sakes but for your own. In the first place, if you help them, they will help you, and in the second, through them you will learn for the benefit of those who are closest to you.

You must know one more thing. Many states of many people are produced artificially—produced artificially not by them but by the Institute. Consequently, sometimes upsetting this state in another hinders the work of the Institute. There is only one salvation: to remember day and night that you are here only for yourself, and everything and everyone round you must either not hinder you, or you must act so that they do not hinder you. You must make use of them as means for attaining your aims.

Yet everything is done here except that. This place has been turned into something worse than ordinary life. Much worse. All day long people are either occupied with scandal, or they blacken one another, or they think things inwardly, judge and consider with each other, finding some sympathetic, some antipathetic; they strike up friendships, collectively or individually,

play mean tricks on each other, concentrate on the bad sides
of each other.

It is no use thinking that there are some here who are better
than others. There are no others here. Here people are neither
clever nor stupid, neither English nor Russian, neither good
nor bad. There are only spoiled automobiles, the same as you.
It is only thanks to these spoiled automobiles that you can attain what you wished for when you came here. Everyone realized this when he came here, but now you have forgotten.
Now it is necessary to awaken to this realization and to come
back to your former idea.

All that I have said can be formulated in two questions: (1)
Why am I here? and (2) Is it worthwhile my remaining?

We never accomplish what we intend doing, in big and little things. We go to si and return to do. Similarly, self-development is impossible without additional force from without and also from within.

(March 25, 1922)

We always use more energy than is necessary, by using unnecessary muscles, by allowing thoughts to revolve and reacting too much with feelings. Relax muscles, use only those necessary, store thoughts and don't express feelings unless you wish. Don't be affected by externals as they are harmless in themselves; we allow ourselves to be hurt.

Hard work is an investment of energy with a good return. Conscious use of energy is a paying investment; automatic use is a wasteful expenditure.

(Prieuré, June 12, 1923)

When one's body revolts against work, fatigue soon sets in; then one must not rest for it would be a victory for the body. When the body desires to rest, don't; when the mind knows it ought to rest, do so, but one must know and distinguish language of body and mind, and be honest.

(March 25, 1922)

Without struggle, no progress and no result. Every breaking of habit produces a change in the machine.

(Prieuré, March 2, 1923)

Energy—sleep

You have probably heard at lectures that in the course of every twenty-four hours our organism produces a definite amount of energy for its existence. I repeat, a definite amount. Yet there is much more of this energy than should be needed for normal expenditure. But since our life is so wrong, we spend the greater part and sometimes the whole of it, and we spend it unproductively.

One of the chief factors consuming energy is our unnecessary movements in everyday life. Later you will see from certain experiments that the greater part of this energy is spent precisely when we make less active movements. For instance, how much energy will a man use up in a day wholly spent in physical labor? A great deal. Yet he will spend even more if he sits still doing nothing. Our large muscles consume less energy because they have become more adapted to momentum, whereas the small muscles consume more because they are less adapted to momentum: they can be set in motion only by force. For instance, as I sit here now I appear to you not to move. But this does not mean I don't spend energy. Every movement, every tension, whether big or small, is possible for me only by spending this energy. Now my arm is tense but I am not moving. Yet I am now spending more energy than if I moved it like this. (*He demonstrates.*)

[115]

It is a very interesting thing, and you must try to understand what I am saying about momentum. When I make a sudden movement, energy flows in, but when I repeat the movement the momentum no longer takes energy. (*He demonstrates.*) At the moment when energy has given the initial push, the flow of energy stops and momentum takes over.

Tension needs energy. If tension is absent, less energy is spent. If my arm is tense, as it is now, a continuous current is required, which means that it is connected with the accumulators. If I now move my arm thus, so long as I do it with pauses, I spend energy.

If a man suffers from chronic tension, then, even if he does nothing, even if he is lying down, he uses more energy than a man who spends a whole day in physical labor. But a man who does not have these small chronic tensions certainly wastes no energy when he does not work or move.

Now we must ask ourselves, are there many among us who are free from this terrible disease? Almost all of us—we are not speaking of people in general but of those present, the rest do not concern us—almost all of us have this delightful habit.

We must bear in mind that this energy about which we now speak so simply and easily, which we waste so unnecessarily and involuntarily, this same energy is needed for the work we intend to do and without which we can achieve nothing.

We cannot get more energy, the inflow of energy will not increase: the machine will remain such as it is created. If the machine is made to produce ten amperes it will go on producing ten amperes. The current can be increased only if all the wires and coils are changed. For instance, one coil represents the nose, another a leg, a third a man's complexion or the size of his stomach. So the machine cannot be changed—its structure will remain as it is. The amount of energy produced is constant: even if the machine is put right, this amount will increase very little.

What we intend to do requires a great deal of energy and much effort. And effort requires much energy. With the kind of efforts we make now, with such lavish expenditure of energy, it is impossible to do what we are now planning to do in our minds.

As we have seen, on the one hand we require a great deal of energy, and on the other our machine is so constructed that it cannot produce more. Where is a way out of this situation? The only way out and the only method and possibility is to economize the energy we have. Therefore if we wish to have a lot of energy when we need it, we must learn to practice economy wherever we can.

One thing is definitely known: one of the chief leakages of energy is due to our involuntary tension. We have many other leakages, but they are all more difficult to repair than the first. So we shall begin with the easiest: to get rid of this leakage and to learn to be able to deal with the others.

A man's sleep is nothing else than interrupted connections between centers. A man's centers never sleep. Since associations are their life, their movement, they never cease, they never stop. A stoppage of associations means death. The movement of associations never stops for an instant in any center, they flow on even in the deepest sleep.

If a man in a waking state sees, hears, senses his thoughts, in half-sleep he also sees, hears, senses his thoughts and he calls this state sleep. Even when he thinks that he absolutely ceases to see or hear, which he also calls sleep, associations go on.

The only difference is in the strength of connections between one center and another.

Memory, attention, observation is nothing more than observation of one center by another, or one center listening to another. Consequently the centers themselves do not need to stop and sleep. Sleep brings the centers neither harm nor profit. So sleep, as it is called, is not meant to give centers a rest. As I have said already, deep sleep comes when the connections between centers are broken. And indeed, deep sleep, complete rest for the machine, is considered to be that sleep when all links, all connections cease to function. We have several centers, so we have as many connections—five connections.

What characterizes our waking state is that all these connections are intact. But if one of them is broken or ceases to function we are neither asleep nor awake.

One link is disconnected—we are no longer awake, neither are we asleep. If two are broken, we are still less awake—but again we are not asleep. If one more is disconnected we are not awake and still not properly asleep, and so on.

Consequently there are different degrees between our waking state and sleep. (Speaking of these degrees, we take an average: there are people who have two connections, others have seven. We have taken five as an example—it is not exact.) Consequently we have not two states, one of sleep and the other of waking, as we think, but several states. Between the most active and intensive state anyone can have and the most passive (somnambulistic sleep) there are definite gradations. If one of the links breaks it is not yet evident on the surface and is unnoticeable to others. There are people whose capacity to move, to walk, to live, stops only when all the connections are broken, and there are other people in whom it is enough to break two connections for them to fall asleep. If we take the range between sleep and waking with seven connections, then there are people who go on living, talking, walking in the third degree of sleep.

Deep states of sleep are the same for all, but intermediate degrees are often subjective.

There are even "prodigies" who are most active when one or several of their connections are broken. If such a state has become customary for a man by education, if he has acquired all he has in this state, his activity is built upon it, and so he cannot be active unless this state is there.

For you personally, the active state is relative—in a certain state you can be active. But there is an objective active state when all the connections are intact, and there is subjective activity in an appropriate state.

So there are many degrees of sleep and waking. Active state is a state when the thinking faculty and the senses work at their full capacity and pressure. We must be interested both in the objective, that is, the genuine, waking state, and in objective sleep. "Objective" means active or passive in actual fact. (It is better not to strive to be but to understand.)

Anyway, everyone must understand that the purpose of sleep is achieved only when all the connections between the centers are broken. Only then can the machine produce what sleep is meant to produce. So the word "sleep" should mean a state when all the links are disconnected.

Deep sleep is a state when we have no dreams or sensations. If people have dreams it means that one of their connections is not broken, since memory, observation, sensation is nothing more than one center observing another. Thus when you see and remember what is happening in you, it means that one center observes another. And if it can observe it follows that there is something through which to observe. And if there is something through which to observe—the connection is not broken.

Consequently, if the machine is in good order, it needs very little time to manufacture that quantity of matter for which sleep is intended; at any rate much less time than we are accustomed to sleep. What we call "sleep" when we sleep for seven to ten hours or God knows how long, is not sleep. The greater part of that time is spent not in sleep but in these transitional states—these unnecessary half-dream states. Some people need many hours to go to sleep and later many hours to come to themselves. If we could fall asleep at once, and as quickly pass from sleep to waking, we would spend on this transition a third or a quarter of the time we are wasting now. But we don't know how to break these connections by ourselves—with us they are broken and reestablished mechanically.

We are slaves of this mechanism. When "it" so pleases, we can pass into another state; when not, we have to lie and wait till "it" gives us leave to rest.

This mechanicalness, this unnecessary slavery and undesirable dependence, has several causes. One of the causes is the chronic state of tension we spoke of in the beginning and which is one of the many causes of the leakage of our reserve energy. So you see how liberation from this chronic tension would serve a double purpose. First, we would save much energy and, second, we would dispense with the useless lying and waiting for sleep.

So you see what a simple thing it is, how easy to attain and how necessary. To free oneself from this tenseness is of tremendous value.

Later I shall give you several exercises for this purpose. I advise you to pay very serious attention to this and to try as hard as you can to get what each of these exercises is expected to give.

It is necessary to learn at all costs not to be tense when tension is not needed. When you sit doing nothing, let the body sleep. When you sleep, sleep in such a way that the whole of you sleeps.

NEW YORK, MARCH 15, 1924

Question: Is there a way of prolonging life?

Answer: Different schools have many theories on prolonging life and there are many systems dealing with this. There are still credulous people who even believe in the existence of the elixir of life.

I shall explain schematically how I understand the question.

Here is a clock. You know that there are different makes of clocks. My clock has a mainspring calculated for twenty-four hours. After twenty-four hours the clock stops working. Clocks of other makes can go a week, a month or even perhaps a year. But the winding mechanism is always calculated for a certain definite time. As it was made by the clockmaker, so it remains.

You may have seen that clocks have a regulator. If it is moved, the clock can work slower or faster. If you take it off, the mainspring may unwind itself very quickly and the spring calculated for twenty-four hours may run out in three or four minutes. So my clock can go a week or a month although its system is calculated for twenty-four hours.

We are like a clock. Our system is already established. Each man has different springs. If heredity is different, the system is different. For example, a system may be calculated for seventy

[121]

years. When the mainspring runs out, life comes to an end. Another man's mechanism may be calculated for a hundred years; it is as though he was made by another craftsman.

So each man has a different time of life. We cannot change our system. Each man remains as he was made and the length of our life cannot be changed; the mainspring runs down and I am finished. In some person the mainspring may last only a week. Length of life is determined at birth and if we think we can change something in this respect it is pure imagination. To do this one would have to change everything: heredity, one's father, even one's grandmother would have to be changed. It is too late for that.

Although our mechanism cannot be changed artificially, there is a possibility to live longer. I said that, instead of twenty-four hours, the mainspring can be made to last a week. Or it can be the other way round: if a system is calculated for fifty years the mainspring can be made to run down in five or six years.

Each man has a mainspring; it is our mechanism. The unwinding of this mainspring is our impressions and associations.

Only, we have two or three coiled springs—as many as there are brains. Brains correspond to springs. For instance, our mind is a spring. Our mental associations have a certain length. Thinking resembles the unwinding of a reel of thread. Each reel has a certain length of thread. When I think, the thread unwinds. My reel has fifty yards of thread, he has a hundred yards. Today I spend two yards, the same tomorrow, and when fifty yards come to an end, my life too comes to an end. The length of thread cannot be changed.

But just as a twenty-four-hour mainspring can be unwound in ten minutes, so life can be spent very quickly. The only difference is that a clock usually has only one spring, whereas a man has several. To each center corresponds one spring of a certain definite length. When one spring has run down, a man can go on living. For instance, his thought is calculated for seventy years, but his feeling only for forty years. So after forty years a man goes on living without feeling. But the un-winding of the spring can be accelerated or retarded.

Nothing can be developed here; the only thing we can do is to economize. Time is proportionate to the flow of associations —it is relative.

You can easily remember such facts. You sit at home, you are calm. You feel that you have been sitting thus five minutes, but the clock shows that an hour has gone by. At another time you are waiting for someone in the street, you are annoyed that he does not come and you think you have been waiting an hour, whereas it was only five minutes. It is because during this time you had many associations; you thought why does he not come, maybe he has been run over, and so on.

The more you concentrate, the quicker the time goes. An hour may pass unnoticed, because if you concentrate you have very few associations, few thoughts, few feelings, and time seems short.

Time is subjective; it is measured by associations. When you sit without concentration, time seems long. Externally time does not exist; it exists for us only internally.

Just as in the thinking center, associations go on in other centers also.

The secret of prolonging life depends on the ability to spend the energy of our centers slowly and only intentionally. Learn to think consciously. This produces economy in the expenditure of energy. Don't dream.

The education of children

Question: There is a way of educating children through suggestion during sleep. Is it any good?

Answer: This kind of suggestion is no better than a gradual poisoning, the destruction of the last vestige of will. Education is a very complicated thing. It must be many-sided. For example, it is wrong to give children nothing but physical exercises.

Generally, education is restricted to the formation of the mind. A child is made to learn poems by heart, like a parrot, without understanding anything, and parents are glad if he can do that. At school he learns things no less mechanically and, after graduating with honors, he nevertheless understands and feels nothing. In the development of his mind, he is as adult as a man of forty, but in his essence he remains a boy of ten. In his mind he is not afraid of anything, but in his essence he is afraid. His morals are purely automatic, purely external. Just as he learns poetry by heart, so he learns morals. But a child's essence, his inner life, is left to itself, without any guidance. If a man is sincere with himself, he has to admit that neither children nor adults have any morals. Our morality is all theoretical and automatic for, if we are sincere, we can see how bad we are.

[124]

Education is nothing but a mask which has nothing to do with nature. People think that one upbringing is better than another, but in actual fact they are all the same. All people are the same, yet each is quick to see a mote in another's eye. We are all blind to our worst faults. If a man is sincere with himself, he enters into another's position and knows that he himself is no better. If you wish to be better, try to help another. But as people are now, they hinder each other and run each other down. Moreover, a man cannot help another, cannot lift another up, because he cannot even help himself.

Before all else you must think of yourself, you must try to lift yourself. You must be an egoist. Egoism is the first station on the way to altruism, to Christianity. But it must be egoism for a good purpose, and this is very difficult. We bring up our children to be ordinary egoists and the present state of things is the result. Yet we must always judge them by ourselves. We know what we are like; we may be sure that with modern education children will be, at best, the same as ourselves.

If you wish your children well, you must first wish yourself well. For if you change, your children too will change. For the sake of their future you must, for a time, forget about them and think about yourself.

If we are satisfied with ourselves, we can continue with a clear conscience to educate our children as we have done up to now. But are you satisfied with yourselves?

We must always start with ourselves and take ourselves as an example, for we cannot see another man through the mask he wears. Only if we know ourselves can we see others, for all people are alike inside and others are the same as we are. They have the same good intentions to be better, but they cannot be; it is just as hard for them; they are equally unhappy, equally full of regrets afterwards. You must forgive what there is in them now and remember the future. If you are sorry for yourself, then for the sake of the future you must be sorry in advance for others.

The greatest sin of all is to continue educating when you

have begun to have doubts about education. If you believe in what you are doing, your responsibility is not as great as when you have begun to doubt.

The law demands that your child shall go to school. Let him. But you, his father, must not be content with school. You know from your own experience that school provides only head knowledge—information. It develops only one center, so you must try to make this information come alive and to fill in the gaps. It is a compromise, but sometimes even a compromise is better than doing nothing.

The problem of sex: There is one important problem in children's education which is never thought about, or spoken about, correctly. A strange feature of modern education is that, in relation to sex, children grow up without guidance; with the result that this whole side is warped and twisted through generations of wrong attitudes. This is the primary cause of many wrong results in life. We see what results from such education. Each one of us knows from his own experience that this important side of life is almost entirely spoiled. It is hard to find a man who is normal in this respect.

This spoiling happens gradually. Manifestations of sex begin in a child from the age of four or five, and without guidance he may easily go wrong. This is the time to begin teaching, and you have your own experience to help you. It is very rare for children to be trained normally in this respect. You are often sorry for the child, but can do nothing. And when he himself begins to understand what is right and what is wrong it is usually too late and the damage is done.

Guiding children in regard to sex is a very tricky thing, because each case requires individual treatment and a thorough knowledge of the child's psychology. If you do not know enough, guiding him is very risky. To explain or forbid something often means to put an idea into his head, to implant an impulse toward the forbidden fruit, to arouse curiosity.

The sex center plays a very great part in our life. Seventy-five percent of our thoughts come from this center, and they color all the rest.

Only the people of central Asia are not abnormal in this respect. There, sex education is part of the religious rites and the results are excellent. There are no sexual evils in that part of the world.

Question: How much should a child be directed?

Answer: Generally speaking, a child's education must be based on the principle that everything must come from his own will. Nothing should be given in a ready-made form. One can only give the idea, one can only guide or even teach indirectly, starting from afar and leading him to the point from something else. I never teach directly, or my pupils would not learn. If I want a pupil to change, I begin from afar, or speak to someone else, and so he learns. For, if something is told to a child directly, he is being educated mechanically and later manifests himself equally mechanically.

Mechanical manifestations and the manifestations of someone who can be called an individual are different and their quality is different. The former are created; the latter create. The former are not creation—it is creation through man and not by him. The result is art which has nothing original. One can see where every line of such a work of art comes from.

Formatory apparatus

I have understood from conversations that people have a wrong idea about one of the centers, and this wrong idea creates many difficulties.

It is about the thinking center, that is, our formatory apparatus. All the stimuli coming from the centers are transmitted to the formatory apparatus, and all the perceptions of centers also are manifested through the formatory apparatus. It is not a center but an apparatus. It is connected with all the centers. In their turn, centers are connected with one another, but these connections are of a special kind. There is a certain degree of subjectivity, a measure of the strength of associations, which determines the possibility of intercommunication between centers. If we take vibrations between 10 and 10,000, then within this range there are many gradations divided into the definite degrees of strength of associations required for each center. Only associations of a certain strength in one center evoke corresponding associations in another; only then can a stimulus be given to corresponding connections in another center.

In the formatory apparatus connections with centers are more sensitive, because all associations reach it. Every local stimulus in the centers, every association, provokes associations in the formatory apparatus.

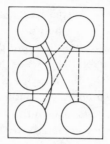

In the case of connections between centers, their sensitivity is determined by a certain degree of subjectivity. Only if the stimulus is strong enough can a corresponding roll° in another center be brought into motion. This can happen only with a very strong stimulus of a particular velocity, the rate of which has already become established in you.

The working arrangements of all these centers are alike. Each one includes a great many smaller ones. Each smaller one is designed for a specific kind of work. So all these centers are alike as to structure, but their essence is different. The four centers are composed of matter which is animate, but the matter of the formatory apparatus is inanimate. The formatory apparatus is simply a machine, just like a typewriter which transmits every impact.

The best way for me to illustrate the formatory apparatus is by an analogy. It is an office with a typist. Every incoming paper comes to her, every client who comes in addresses himself to her. She replies to everything. The answers she gives are qualified by the fact that, in herself, she is only an employee, she does not know anything. But she has instructions, books, files and dictionaries on the shelves. If she has the wherewithal to look up some particular information she does so and replies accordingly; if she hasn't, she does not answer.

This factory also has four partners who sit in four different rooms. These partners communicate with the outside world

° or tape

through her. They are connected with her office by telephone. If one of them phones to her and says something, she has to pass it on further. Now each of the four directors has a different code. Suppose one of them sends her something to be transmitted exactly. Since the message is in code, she cannot pass it on as it is, for a code is something arbitrarily agreed upon. She has in her office a quantity of stereotypes, forms, and signs, which have accumulated over the years. According to whom she is in contact with, she consults a book, decodes and transmits.

If the partners want to talk to each other there is no means of communication between them. They are connected by telephone, but this telephone can work only in good weather and in such conditions of calm and quiet as seldom occur. Since such conditions are rare, they send messages through the central exchange, that is, the office. Since each one has his own code, it is the typist's job to decode and recode these messages. Consequently the decoding depends on this employee who has no interest or concern in the business. As soon as the daily grind is over she goes home. Her decoding depends on how well she is educated; typists can be of different education. One may be a fool, another may be a good business woman. There is an established routine in the office and the typist acts according to it. If she needs a certain code, she has to bring out one or another stereotype, so she uses whichever of the more frequently used stereotypes happens to be handy.

This office is a modern one and has a number of mechanical appliances, so the typist's work is very easy. She is very rarely obliged to use a typewriter. There are all sorts of inventions, both mechanical and semi-mechanical; for every kind of inquiry there are ready-made labels which are immediately affixed.

Then of course there is the almost chronic character of all typists. Usually they are young girls of a romantic disposition who spend their time reading novels and dealing with their personal correspondence. A typist is usually coquettish. She constantly looks at herself in the mirror, powders her face and busies herself with her own affairs, for her bosses are seldom there. Often she does not catch exactly what is said, but absentmindedly presses the wrong button which brings out one stereotype instead of another. What does she care—the directors come so seldom!

Just as the directors communicate with each other through her, so they do with people outside. Everything that comes in or goes out has to be decoded and recoded. It is her job to decode and recode all communications between the directors, and then forward them to their destination. It is the same with all incoming correspondence: if it is addressed to one of the directors, it is forwarded by her in the appropriate code. However, she often makes mistakes and sends something in the wrong code to one of them. He gets it and understands nothing. This is an approximate picture of the state of affairs.

This office is our formatory apparatus, and the typist represents our education, our automatically mechanical views, local clichés, theories and opinions that have been formed in us. The typist has nothing in common with the centers, and indeed not even with the formatory apparatus. But she works there, and I have explained to you what this girl means. Education has nothing to do with centers. A child is brought up thus: "If someone is shaking hands with you, you must always stand like this." All this is purely mechanical—in *this* case, you must do *that*. And once established so it remains. An adult is the same. If someone treads on his corn he reacts always in the same manner. Adults are like children, and children are like adults: all of them react. The machine works and will go on working in the same way a thousand years hence.

With time a great quantity of labels accumulates on the office shelves. The longer a man lives, the more labels there are in the office. It is so arranged that all labels of a similar kind are kept in one cupboard. So when an inquiry comes in, the typist begins to search for a suitable label. To do this she must take them out, look through and sort them until she finds the right one. A great deal depends on the tidiness of the typist and in what state she keeps her files of labels. Some typists are methodical; others not so methodical. Some keep them sorted out, others don't. One may put an incoming inquiry in a wrong drawer, others not. One finds a label at once, another looks for a long time and mixes them all up while searching.

Our so-called thoughts are nothing more than these labels taken out of the cupboard. What we call thoughts are not thoughts, we have no thoughts: we have different labels, short, abbreviated, long—but nothing except labels. These labels are shifted from one place to another. Inquiries coming from outside are what we receive as impressions. These manifestations, inquiries, come not only from without but also from different places within. All this has to be recoded.

All this chaos is what we call our thoughts and associations. At the same time a man does have thoughts. Every center thinks. These thoughts, if there are any and if they reach the formatory apparatus, reach it only in the form of stimuli and are then reconstructed, but the reconstruction is mechanical. And this is so in the best cases, for as a rule some centers have hardly any means of communicating with the formatory apparatus. Owing to faulty connections, messages are either not transmitted at all or are transmitted in distorted form. But this does not prove the absence of thought. In all centers work goes on, there are thoughts and associations, but they do not reach the formatory apparatus and so are not manifested. Neither are they sent on in another direction—that is, from the formatory apparatus to the centers—and for the same reason they cannot get there from outside.

Everyone has centers; the difference lies only in the amount of material they contain. Some have more, others less. Everyone has some, the difference is only in the quantity. But the centers are the same in everyone.

A man is born like an empty cupboard or storehouse. Then material begins to accumulate. The machine works alike in everyone; the properties of the centers are the same, but, owing to their nature and the conditions of life, the links, the connections between centers, differ in degrees of sensitivity, coarseness or fineness.

The most primitive and most accessible is the connection between the moving center and the formatory apparatus. This connection is the coarsest, the most "audible," the speediest, thickest and best. It is like a large pipe (I mean here not the center itself but the connection). It is the quickest to form, and the quickest to be filled. The second is considered to be the connection with the sex center. The third—the connection with the emotional center. The fourth—the connection with the thinking center.

So the amount of material and the degree of functioning of these connections stand in this gradation. The first connection exists and functions in all men; associations are received and manifested. The second connection, the one with the sex center, exists in the majority of men. Consequently most people live with the first and second centers—their whole life, all their perceptions and manifestations come from these centers and originate in them. People whose emotional center is connected with the formatory apparatus are in the minority, and in their case all their life and manifestations proceed through it. But there is hardly anyone in whom the connection with the thinking center works.

If a man's manifestations in life are to be classified according to their quality and cause, we find the following proportion: 50 percent of his vital manifestations and perceptions belong to the moving center, 40 percent to the sex center and 10 percent to the emotional center. Yet at a superficial glance we are accustomed to attach a high value to these manifestations of the emotional center and give high-sounding names to their comings and goings, allotting a lofty place to them.

Anyway, we have so far been speaking of the situation at its best. With us things are still worse. If the thinking center is of quality No. 1; the emotional, quality No. 2; the sex center, quality No. 3; and the moving, quality No. 4, then at best we

have very little of the second quality, more of the third quality
and a lot of the fourth quality, taking it from the point of view
of true value. In actual fact, however, over 75 percent of our
vital manifestations and perceptions take place with no
connection whatever, entirely through this hired employee
who, when she goes out, leaves behind only a machine.

I began with one thing and ended by speaking of another.
Let us return to what I meant to say about the formatory apparatus.

For some reason those who come to lectures call it also a
center. But in order to understand what follows it is necessary
to make clear that it is not a center. It is simply a certain
organ, although it too is in the brain. Both in its matter and its
structure it is completely different from what we call an animate center. These animate centers, if we take them singly,
are in themselves animals and they live like corresponding animals. This one is the brain of a worm; that one the first brain
of a sheep. There are animals which have something similar.
Here brains of different degrees of fineness are collected together in one. There exist one-brained organizations and two-
brained organizations. So that each one of these brains in an
individual organization acts as a moving factor—as a soul.
They are independent. Even if they live in one and the same
place, they can and do exist independently. Each has its own
properties. Some people live animated now by one, now by another. Each brain has a definite, independent, specific existence. In short, according to the quality of its matter, each can
be called an individual entity, a soul.

Cohesion, existence, has its own laws. From the point of
view of its materiality, in accordance with the law of cohesion,
the formatory apparatus is an organism. In the centers, life, associations, influence and existence are psychical, whereas in
the formatory apparatus all its properties, qualities, its existence, are organic.

(Injury, sickness, treatment of sickness, disharmony are

physical. Effect, cause, quality, state, change are psychical.)

To those who have heard about densities of intelligence I can say that the sex center and the moving center have a corresponding density of intelligence, whereas the formatory apparatus does not have this property. The action of these centers and their reaction are both psychical, whereas in the formatory apparatus they are both material. Consequently our thinking, our so-called thoughts—if the cause and effect of this thinking lie in the formatory apparatus—are material. No matter how highly varied our thinking may be, no matter what label it bears, what guise it assumes, what high-sounding name it has, the value of this thinking is simply material. And material things are, for instance, bread, coffee, the fact that someone has trodden on my corn, looking sideways or straight, scratching my back, and so on. If this material, such as pain in the corn, etc., were absent, there would be no thinking.

Body, essence and personality

When a man is born, three separate machines are born with him which continue to form till his death. These machines have nothing in common with one another: they are our body, our essence and our personality. Their formation does not depend on us in any way. Their future development, the development of each one separately, depends on the data a man possesses and the data which surround him, such as environment, circumstances, geographical conditions and so on.

For the body these data are heredity, geographical conditions, food and movement. They do not affect personality.

In the course of a man's life, personality is formed exclusively through what a man hears and through reading.

Essence is purely emotional. It consists of what is received from heredity before the formation of personality, and later, only those sensations and feelings among which a man lives. What comes after merely depends on the transition.

So the body begins to develop in each man subjectively. The development of all three starts from the first days of a man's life. All three develop independently of one another. Thus it may happen, for instance, that the body begins its life in favorable conditions, on healthy soil and, as a result, is brave; but this does not necessarily mean that the man's essence is of a similar character. In the same conditions, essence may be weak and cowardly. A man may have a brave body contrasting with a cowardly essence. Essence does not necessarily develop parallel with the development of the body. A man may be very strong and healthy, yet as timid as a rabbit.

The center of gravity of the body, its soul, is the moving center. The center of gravity of the essence is the emotional center, and the center of gravity of the personality is the thinking center. The soul of the essence is the emotional center. Just as a man may have a healthy body and a cowardly essence, so personality may be bold and essence timid. Take for instance a man of common sense; he has studied and knows that hallucinations can occur; he knows that they cannot be real. So in his personality he does not fear them, but his essence is afraid. If his essence sees a phenomenon of this kind it cannot help being afraid. Development of one center does not depend on the development of another, and one center cannot transfer its results to another.

It is impossible to say positively that a man is such or such. One of his centers may be brave, another cowardly; one good, another wicked; one may be sensitive, another very coarse; one gives readily, another is slow in giving or quite incapable of giving. So it is impossible to say: good, brave, strong or wicked.

As we have said already, each of the three machines is the whole chain, the whole system relating to one, to another, to a third. In itself each machine is very complicated but is brought into motion very simply. The more complicated the parts of the machine, the fewer the levers. Each human machine is complex, but the number of levers in each one separately may differ—in one, more levers, in another, fewer.

In the course of life one machine may form many levers for bringing it into motion, whereas another may be brought into motion by a small number of levers. Time for the formation of levers is limited. In its turn this time also depends on heredity and geographical conditions. On an average, new levers are formed up to seven or eight years of age; later, up to the age of 14 or 15, they are capable of alterations; but after 16 or 17 years of age levers are neither formed nor altered. So later in life only those levers act which have been already formed. This is how things are in ordinary normal life, no matter how much a man may be puffing and blowing. This is true even as regards man's capacity to learn. New things can be learned only up to the age of 17; what can be learned later is only learning in quotation marks, that is, merely a reshuffling of the old. At first this may seem difficult to understand.

Each individual man with his levers depends on his heredity and the place, social circle and circumstances in which he was born and grew up. The workings of all three centers, or souls, are similar. Their construction is different, but their manifestation is the same.

The first movements are recorded. Records of the movements of the body are purely subjective. This recording is like that of a phonograph disc—at first, up to three months, it is very sensitive; then after four months it becomes less sensitive; after a year, still weaker. At first even the sound of breathing can be heard, a week later one can hear nothing below a low-voiced conversation. It is the same with the human brain: at first it is very receptive and every new movement is recorded. As a final result one man may have many postures, another only a few. For instance, one man may have acquired 55 postures while the possibility of recording them lasted, while another man, living in the same conditions, may have obtained 250. These levers, these postures, are formed in each center according to the same laws, and remain there for the rest of a man's life. The difference among these postures is only in the way they are recorded. Take, for instance, postures of the moving center. Up to a certain time postures become formed in every man. Then they stop being formed, but those that are formed remain till his death. Their number is limited, so whatever a man may be doing he will use these same postures. If he wishes to play one or another role, he will use a combina-

tion of postures he already has, for he will never have any others. In ordinary life there can be no new postures. Even if a
man wishes to be an actor his position will be the same in this
respect.

The difference between sleep and waking of the body is that
when a shock comes from outside in sleep, it does not excite,
does not produce associations in the corresponding brain.

Let us say a man happens to be tired. The first shock is
given. Some lever begins to move mechanically. Equally mechanically it touches another lever and makes it move; that
lever touches a third, the third a fourth, and so on. This is
what we call associations of the body. The other machines also
have postures and they are brought into motion in the same
way.

Besides the central, independently working machines—
body, personality and essence—we also have soulless manifestations which take place outside of the centers. In order to understand this, it is very important to note that we divide
postures of body and feeling into two kinds: 1) direct manifestations of any center, and 2) purely mechanical manifestations
arising outside centers. For instance, the movement of lifting
up my arm is initiated by the center. But in another man it
may be initiated outside the center. Suppose a similar process is taking place in the emotional center, such as joy, sorrow, vexation, jealousy. At one time a strong posture may have
coincided with one of these emotional postures and the two
postures have thus given rise to a new mechanical posture.
This happens independently of centers, mechanically.

When I spoke of machines I called normal work a manifestation of a man—which implies all three centers taken together. This is his manifestation. But owing to abnormal life
some people have other levers, which become formed outside
centers and which provoke movement independently of the
soul. It can be in the flesh, the muscles, anywhere.

Movements, manifestations, perceptions by separate centers
are manifestations of centers but not of man, if we bear in

mind that man consists of three centers. The capacity to feel joy, sorrow, cold, heat, hunger, tiredness is in each center. These postures exist in every center and may be small or big and different in quality. We shall speak later about how this happens in each separate center and how to know to which center they belong. For the moment you must bear in mind and realize one thing: you must learn to distinguish the manifestations of man from the manifestations of centers. When people speak of a man, they say he is wicked, clever, a fool —all this is he. But they cannot say that this is John or Simon. We are accustomed to saying "he." But we must become used to saying "he" in the sense of he as body, he as essence, he as personality.

Suppose in a given case we represent essence as 3 units: 3 represents the number of postures. In the case of this man's body the number is 4. The head is represented by 6. Thus, when we speak of 6 we do not refer to the whole man. We must evaluate him by 13, for 13 is his manifestations, his perception. When it is the head alone, it would be 6. The important thing is not to evaluate him by only 6 but by 13. The total is what defines him. A man should be able to give a total of 30 for everything taken together. This figure can be obtained only if each center can give a certain corresponding number—for instance, 12 + 10 + 8. Let us suppose that this figure 30 represents the manifestation of a man, a householder. If we find that one center must necessarily give 12, it must contain certain corresponding postures which would produce 12. If one unit is missing and it gives only 11, 30 cannot be obtained. If there is a total of only 29 it is not a man, if we call a man one whose sum-total is 30.

When we spoke about centers and a harmonious development of centers, we meant that in order to become such a man, to be able to produce what we were speaking about, the following is necessary. At the very beginning we said that our centers are formed independently of one another and have nothing in common with each other. But there should be a correlation between them, because the sum-total of manifestations can be obtained only from the three together, and not from only one. If 30 is correctly a true manifestation of man and this 30 is produced by three centers in a corresponding correlation, then it is imperative that the centers should be in this correlation. It should be so, but in reality it is not so. Each center is separate (I speak of those present), they have no proper relationship to one another and so they are disharmonious.

For example, one has a great many postures in one center, another in another center. If we take each type separately, the sum-total of everyone will be different. If, according to the principle, there should be 12, 10, and 8, but only 10 and 8 are there, and instead of 12 there is 0, the result is 18 and not 30.

Take some substance—say, bread. It requires a definite proportion of flour, water and fire. It is bread only when the ingredients are in the right proportion, and similarly with man, to obtain the figure 30, each source must contribute a corresponding quality and quantity. If J. has much flour, that is, physical postures, but no water or fire, it is simply flour and not an individual, not bread. She (O.) produces water (feeling), she has many postures. But no bread can be got from water— again it is worth nothing; the sea is full of water. L. has much fire but no flour or water—again it is worth nothing. If they could be put together, the result would be 30—an individual. As they are, they are only pieces of meat; but the three together would give 30 as manifestation. Could she say "I"? "We," not "I." She produces water, yet she says "I." Each of these three machines is, as it were, a man. And all the three fit into one another. Man consists of three men; each has a different character, different nature and suffers from lack of correspondence with the others. Our aim must be to organize them so as to make them correspond. But before beginning to organize them and before thinking of a manifestation worth 30, let us pause to see consciously that these three machines of ours are indeed at variance with one another. They are not acquainted with one another. Not only do they not listen to one another, but if one of them begs the other very hard to do something, and knows how it should be done, the other either cannot or will not do it.

As it is late, we must put off the rest till another time. By then you may perhaps learn to do!

Essence and personality

In order to understand better the meaning of external and internal considering, you must understand that every man has two completely separate parts, as it were two different men, in him. These are his essence and his personality.

Essence is I—it is our heredity, type, character, nature.

Personality is an accidental thing—upbringing, education, points of view—everything external. It is like the clothes you wear, your artificial mask, the result of your upbringing, of the influence of your surroundings, opinions consisting of information and knowledge which change daily, one annulling the other.

Today you are convinced of one thing—you believe it and want it. Tomorrow, under another influence, your belief, your desires become different. All the material constituting your personality may be completely changed artificially or accidentally with a change in your surrounding conditions and place —and this in a very short time.

Essence does not change. For instance, I have a swarthy skin, and I shall remain as I was born. This belongs to my type.

Here, when we speak of development and change, we speak of essence. Our personality remains a slave; it may be changed very quickly, even in half an hour. For instance, by hypnosis it is possible to change your convictions. This is because they are alien, not your own. But what we have in our essence is our own.

We always consider in essence, mechanically. Every influence mechanically evokes a corresponding considering. Mechanically, you may like me, and so, mechanically, you register this impression of me. But it is not you. It does not come from consciousness; it happens mechanically. Sympathy and antipathy is a question of correspondence of types. Inwardly you like me, and although in your mind you know that I am bad, that I do not deserve your liking, you cannot dislike me. Or again: you may see that I am good, but you do not like me —and so it remains.

But we have the possibility not to consider inwardly. At present you cannot do this, because your essence is a function. Our essence consists of many centers, but our personality has only one center, the formatory apparatus.

Remember our example of the carriage, horse and driver. Our essence is the horse. It is precisely the horse that should not consider. But even if you realize this, the horse does not, because it doesn't understand your language. You cannot order it about, teach it, tell it not to consider, not to react, not to respond.

With your mind you wish not to consider, but first of all you must learn the language of the horse, its psychology, in order to be able to talk to it. Then you will be able to do what the mind, what logic, wishes. But if you try to teach it now, you will not be able to teach it or to change anything in a hundred years; it will remain an empty wish. At present you have only two words at your disposal: "right" and "left." If you jerk the reins the horse will go here or there, and even then not always, but only when it is full. But if you start telling it something it will only keep on driving away flies with its tail, and you may imagine that it understands you. Before our nature was spoiled, all four in this team—horse, cart, driver, master—

were one; all the parts had a common understanding, all worked together, labored, rested, fed, at the same time. But the language has been forgotten, each part has become separate and lives cut off from the rest. Now, at times, it is necessary for them to work together, but it is impossible—one part wants one thing, another part something else.

The point is to reestablish what has been lost, not to acquire anything new. This is the purpose of development. For this one must learn to discriminate between essence and personality, and to separate them. When you have learned to do this you will see what to change and how. Meantime, you have only one possibility—to study. You are weak, you are dependent—you are slaves. It is difficult to break all at once the habits accumulated in years. Later it will be possible to replace certain habits with others. These will also be mechanical. Man is always dependent on external influences; only, some influences hinder, other influences do not.

To begin with, it is necessary to prepare conditions for work. There are many conditions. At present you can only observe and collect material which will be useful for work; you cannot distinguish where your manifestations come from— from essence or from personality. But if you look carefully you may understand afterwards. While you are collecting material you cannot see that. This is because ordinarily man has only one attention, directed on what he is doing. His mind does not see his feelings, and vice versa.

Many things are necessary for observing. The first is sincerity with oneself. And this is very difficult. It is much easier to be sincere with a friend. Man is afraid to see something bad, and if, by accident, looking deep down, he sees his own bad, he sees his nothingness. We have the habit of driving away thoughts about ourselves because we fear the gnawings of conscience. Sincerity may be the key which will open the door through which one part can see another part. With sincerity man may look and see something. Sincerity with oneself is very difficult, for a thick crust has grown over essence. Each year a man puts on new clothes, a new mask, again and again. All this should be gradually removed—one should free oneself, uncover oneself. Until man uncovers himself he cannot see.

In the beginning of the work one exercise is very useful, for it helps one to see oneself, to collect material. This exercise is: entering into the position of another. This should be undertaken as a task. To explain what I mean, let us take a simple fact. I know that you need a hundred dollars by tomorrow, but you have not got it. You try to get it and fail. You are sad. Your thoughts and feelings are occupied with this problem. In the evening you are here at the lecture. Half of you keeps thinking about the money. You are absentminded, nervous. If I am rude to you on some other occasion you will not be as angry as you are today. Perhaps tomorrow, when you have the money, you will laugh at the same thing. If I see that you are angry, then, knowing that you are not always like that, I will try to enter into your position. I ask myself how I would act in your place if someone were rude to me. If I ask this question often I shall soon understand that if rudeness angers or hurts another there is always some reason for it at that moment. I shall soon understand that all people are alike—that no one is always bad or always good. We are all alike. Just as I change so does another. If you realize this and remember it, if you think and do your task at the right time, you will see many new things in yourself and your surroundings, things you have not seen before. This is the first step.

The second step is—practice in concentration. Through this exercise you can achieve another thing. Self-observation is very difficult, but it can give much material. If you remember how you manifest yourself, how you react, how you feel, what you want—you may learn many things. Sometimes you may distinguish at once what is thought, what is feeling, what is body.

Each part is under different influences; and if we free ourselves of one we become slaves of another. For example, I can be free in my mind, but I cannot change the emanations of my body—my body responds differently. A man sitting next to me affects me by his emanations. I know that I should be polite but I feel antipathy. Each center has its own spheres of emanations, and at times there is no escaping them. It is very good to combine this exercise of putting oneself in another's place with self-observation.

But we always forget. We remember only afterwards. At the necessary moment our attention is occupied, for example, with the fact that we don't like the man and cannot help feeling it. But facts should not be forgotten, they should be recorded in the memory. The taste of an experience remains only for a time. Without attention, manifestations vanish. Things should be noted in the memory, otherwise you will forget. And what we want is not to forget. There are many things that are seldom repeated. Accidentally you see something, but if you don't commit it to memory you will forget and lose it. If you want "to know America" you must imprint it on your memory. Sitting in your room you will not see anything: you should observe in life. In your room you cannot develop the master. A man may be strong in a monastery, but weak in life, and we want strength for life. For instance, in a monastery, a man could be without food for a week, but in life he cannot be without food even for three hours. What then is the good of his exercises?

Separation of oneself from oneself

As long as a man does not separate himself from himself he can achieve nothing, and no one can help him.

To govern oneself is a very difficult thing—it is a problem for the future; it requires much power and demands much work. But this first thing, to separate oneself from oneself, does not require much strength, it only needs desire, serious desire, the desire of a grown-up man. If a man cannot do it, it shows that he lacks the desire of a grown-up man. Consequently it proves that there is nothing for him here. What we do here can only be a doing suitable for grown-up men.

Our mind, our thinking, has nothing in common with us, with our essence—no connection, no dependence. Our mind lives by itself and our essence lives by itself. When we say "to separate oneself from oneself" it means that the mind should stand apart from the essence. Our weak essence can change at any moment, for it is dependent on many influences: on food, on our surroundings, on time, on the weather, and on a multitude of other causes. But the mind depends on very few influences and so, with a little effort, it can be kept in the desired direction. Every weak man can give the desired direction to his mind. But he has no power over his essence; great power is

[148]

required to give direction to essence and keep essence to it. (Body and essence are the same devil.) Man's essence does not depend on him: it can be good-tempered or bad-tempered, irritable, cheerful or sad, excitable or placid. All these reactions may happen independently of him. A man may be cross because he has eaten something which has produced this effect.

If a man has no special attainments, nothing can be demanded of him. Therefore one cannot expect of him more than he has. From a purely practical point of view, a man is certainly not responsible in this respect; it is not his fault that he is what he is. So I take this fact into consideration, for I know that you cannot expect from a weak man something that requires strength. One can make demands of a man only in accordance with the strength he has to fulfill them.

Naturally the majority of people present are here because they lack this strength and have come here to acquire it. This means that they wish to be strong, and so strength is not expected of them.

But I am speaking now of another part of us, the mind. Speaking of the mind I know that each of you has enough strength, each of you can have the power and capacity to act not as he now acts.

The mind is capable of functioning independently, but it also has the capacity of becoming identified with the essence, of becoming a function of the essence. In the majority of those present, the mind does not try to be independent but is merely a function.

I repeat, every grown-up man can achieve this; everyone who has a serious desire can do it. But no one tries.

And so, in spite of the fact that they have been here so long, in spite even of the desire they had for so long before coming here—they still stand on a level below that of a householder, that is, the level of a man who never intended to do anything.

I repeat again: at present we are not capable of controlling our states, and so it cannot be demanded of us. But when we acquire this capacity, corresponding demands will be made.

In order to understand better what I mean, I shall give you an example: now, in a calm state, not reacting to anything or anyone, I decide to set myself the task of establishing a good relationship with Mr. B., because I need him for business purposes and can do what I wish only with his help. But I dislike Mr. B. for he is a very disagreeable man. He understands nothing. He is a blockhead. He is vile, anything you like. I am so made that these traits affect me. Even if he merely looks at me, I become irritated. If he talks nonsense, I am beside myself. I am only a man, so I am weak and cannot persuade myself that I need not be annoyed—I shall go on being annoyed.

Yet I can control myself, depending on how serious my desire is to gain the end I wish to gain through him. If I keep to this purpose, to this desire, I shall be able to do so. No matter how annoyed I may be, this state of wishing will be in my mind. No matter how furious, how beside myself I am, in a corner of my mind I shall still remember the task I set myself. My mind is unable to restrain me from anything, unable to make me feel this or that toward him, but it is able to remember. I say to myself: "You need him, so don't be cross or rude to him." It could even happen that I would curse him, or hit him, but my mind would continue to pluck at me, reminding me that I should not do so. But the mind is powerless to do anything.

This is precisely what anyone who has a serious desire not to identify himself with his essence can do. This is what is meant by "separating the mind from the essence."

And what happens when the mind becomes merely a function? If I am annoyed, if I lose my temper, I shall think, or rather "it" will think, in accordance with this annoyance, and I shall see everything in the light of the annoyance. To hell with it!

And so I say that with a serious man—a simple, ordinary man without any extraordinary powers, but a grown-up man —whatever he decides, whatever problem he has set himself, that problem will always remain in his head. Even if he cannot

achieve it in practice, he will always keep it in his mind. Even
if he is influenced by other considerations, his mind will not
forget the problem he has set himself. He has a duty to perform and, if he is honest, he will strive to perform it, because
he is a grown-up man.

No one can help him in this remembering, in this separation
of oneself from oneself. A man must do it for himself. Only
then, from the moment a man has this separation, can another
man help him. Consequently, only from that moment can the
Institute be of any use to him, if he came to the Institute seeking this help.

You have probably heard things said at lectures on the subject of what a man wishes. I can say about the majority of
those who are here now that they do not know what they
wish, they do not know why they are here. They have no basic
desire. At every moment each one wishes something, but in
him "it" wishes.

I have just given as an example that I wish to borrow money
from Mr. B. I can get what I wish only by making this desire
primary, the chief thing I want. And so, if each of you wishes
something and the Institute knows what he wishes, the Institute will be able to help. But if a man has a million desires,
and no predominant one, then not a single desire can be satisfied, for years are needed to give one thing, and to give a million things. . . . It is true that it is not easy to wish; but the
mind must always remember what it wishes.

The only difference between a child and a grown-up man is
in the mind. All the weaknesses are there, beginning with hunger, with sensitivity, with naiveté; there is no difference. The
same things are in a child and in a grown-up man: love, hate,
everything. Functions are the same, receptivity is the same,
equally they react, equally they are given to imaginary fears.
In short there is no difference. The only difference is in the
mind: we have more material, more logic than a child.

Now again as an example: A. looked at me and called me a
fool. I lost my temper and went for him. A child does the

same. But a grown-up man, who will be just as angry, will not hit him; he will restrain himself. For if he does hit him, the police will come and he is afraid of what other people will think; they will say: "What an uncontrolled man!" Or I refrain for fear he will run away from me tomorrow, and I need him for my work. In short, there are thousands of thoughts that may stop me or fail to stop me. But still these thoughts will be there.

A child has no logic, no material, and because of that his mind is only function. His mind will not stop to think—with him it will be "it thinks," but this "it thinks" will be colored with hate, which means identification.

There are no definite degrees between children and adults. Length of life does not mean maturity. A man may live to a hundred and yet remain a child; he may grow tall and be a child all the same, if we mean by a "child" one who has no independent logic in his mind. A man can be called "grown-up" only from the moment his mind has acquired this quality. So, from this point of view, it can be said that the Institute is only for grown-up people. Only a grown-up person can derive any profit from it. A boy or a girl of eight can be grown-up, and a man of sixty can be a child. The Institute cannot make people grown-up; they have to be grown-up before they come to the Institute. Those who are in the Institute must be grown-up, and by this I mean grown-up not in their essence but in their mind.

Before going any further it is necessary to make clear what each person wishes, and what he or she can give to the Institute.

The Institute can give very little. The program of the Institute, the power of the Institute, the aim of the Institute, the possibilities of the Institute can be expressed in few words: the Institute can help one to be able to be a Christian. Simple! That is all! It can do so only if a man has this desire, and a man will have this desire only if he has a place where constant desire is present. Before being able, one must wish.

Thus there are three periods: to wish, to be able, and to be.

The Institute is the means. Outside the Institute it is possible to wish and to be; but here, to be able.

The majority of those present here call themselves Christians. Practically all are Christians in quotation marks. Let us examine this question like grown-up men.

—Dr. X., are you a Christian? What do you think, should one love one's neighbor or hate him? Who can love like a Christian? It follows that to be a Christian is impossible. Christianity includes many things; we have taken only one of them, to serve as an example. Can you love or hate someone to order?

Yet Christianity says precisely this, to love all men. But this is impossible. At the same time it is quite true that it is necessary to love. First one must be able, only then can one love. Unfortunately, with time, modern Christians have adopted the second half, to love, and lost view of the first, the religion which should have preceded it.

It would be very silly for God to demand from man what he cannot give.

Half of the world is Christian, the other half has other religions. For me, a sensible man, this makes no difference; they are the same as the Christian. Therefore it is possible to say that the whole world is Christian, the difference is only in name. And it has been Christian not only for one year but for thousands of years. There were Christians long before the advent of Christianity. So common sense says to me: "For so many years men have been Christians—how can they be so foolish as to demand the impossible?"

But it is not like that. Things have not always been as they are now. Only recently have people forgotten the first half, and because of that have lost the capacity for being able. And so it became indeed impossible.

Let every one ask himself, simply and openly, whether he can love all men. If he has had a cup of coffee, he loves; if not, he does not love. How can that be called Christianity?

In the past not all men were called Christians. Some members of the same family were called Christians, others pre-Christians, still others were called non-Christians. So in one and the same family there could be the first, the second and the third. But now all call themselves Christians. It is naive, dishonest, unwise and despicable to wear this name without justification.

A Christian is a man who is able to fulfill the Commandments.

A man who is able to do all that is demanded of a Christian, both with his mind and his essence, is called a Christian without quotation marks. A man who, in his mind, wishes to do all that is demanded of a Christian, but can do so only with his mind and not with his essence, is called pre-Christian. And a man who can do nothing, even with his mind, is called a non-Christian.

Try to understand what I wish to convey by all this. Let your understanding be deeper and broader.

The stop exercise

The "stop" exercise is obligatory for all the students of the Institute. In this exercise, at the command "stop," or at a previously arranged signal, every student must instantly stop all movement, wherever he may be and whatever he may be doing. Whether in the middle of rhythmic movements or in the ordinary life of the Institute, at work or at table, he not only must stop his movements but must retain the expression of his face, smile, glance and the tension of all the muscles of his body in exactly the state they were in at the command "stop." He must keep his eyes fixed on the exact spot at which they happened to be looking at the moment of the command. While he is in this state of arrested movement, the student must also arrest the flow of his thoughts, not admitting any new thoughts whatever. And he must concentrate the whole of his attention on observing the tension of the muscles in the various parts of his body, guiding the attention from one part of the body to another, taking care that the muscular tension does not alter, neither decreasing nor increasing.

In a man thus arrested and remaining motionless, there are no postures. This is simply a movement interrupted at the moment of passage from one posture to another.

Generally we pass from one posture to another so rapidly

that we do not notice the attitudes we take in passing. The "stop" exercise gives us the possibility of seeing and feeling our own body in postures and attitudes which are entirely unaccustomed and unnatural to it.

Every race, every nation, every epoch, every country, every class and every profession has its own limited number of postures from which it can never depart and which represents the particular style of the given epoch, race or profession. Every man, according to his individuality, adopts a certain number of postures from the style available to him, and therefore each individual has an extremely limited repertory of postures. This can easily be seen, for instance in bad art, when an artist, accustomed mechanically to represent the style and movements of one race or one class, attempts to portray another race or class.

Rich material in this respect is given by illustrated newspapers, where we may often see Orientals with movements and attitudes of English soldiers, or peasants with the movements and postures of operatic singers.

The style of the movements and postures of every epoch, every race and every class is indissolubly connected with distinctive forms of thought and of feeling. And they are so closely bound together that a man can change neither the form of his thought nor the form of his feeling without having changed his repertory of postures.

The forms of thought and feeling may be called postures of thought and feeling. Every man has a definite number of intellectual and emotional postures, just as he has a definite number of moving postures; and his moving, intellectual and emotional postures are all interconnected. Thus, a man can never get away from his own repertory of intellectual and emotional postures unless his moving postures are changed.

Psychological analysis and the study of the psychomotor functions, applied in a certain manner, demonstrate that each of our movements, voluntary or involuntary, is an unconscious transition from one automatically fixed posture to another, equally automatic. It is an illusion that our movements are voluntary; in reality they are automatic. Our thoughts and feelings are equally automatic. And the automatism of our thoughts and of our feelings is definitely connected with the automatism of our movements. One cannot be changed without the other. And if, for instance, the attention of a man is concentrated on changing the automatism of thought, his habitual movements and postures will obstruct the new mode of thought by evoking old habitual associations.

We do not recognize to what an extent the intellectual, emotional and moving functions are mutually dependent, although, at the same time, we can be aware of how much our moods and emotional states depend on our movements and postures. If a man assumes a posture that corresponds, in him, to a feeling of grief or dejection, then within a short time he will actually feel grief or dejection. Fear, indifference, aversion and so on may be created by artificial changes of posture.

Since all the functions of man—intellectual, emotional and moving—possess their own definite repertory of postures and are in constant reciprocal action, it follows that a man can never depart from his own repertory.

But the methods of work in the Institute for the Harmonious Development of Man offer a possibility to depart from this circle of innate automatism, and one of the means for this, especially at the beginning of work upon oneself, is the "stop" exercise. Nonmechanical study of oneself is possible only with the application of the "stop" exercise.

The movement that has been begun is broken off at the sudden command or signal. The body becomes motionless and fixed in mid-passage from one posture to another, in an attitude in which it never stops in ordinary life. By perceiving himself in this state, that is, in the state of an unaccustomed posture, a man looks at himself from new points of view, sees and observes himself anew. In this posture, not customary for him, he can think anew, feel anew, and know himself anew. In this manner the circle of the old automatism is broken. The body vainly struggles to take the habitual posture comfortable for it. The will of the man, brought into action by the order "stop," prevents this. The "stop" exercise is simultaneously an exercise for the will, for the attention, for thought, for feeling and for movements.

But it is necessary to understand that to activate the will strongly enough to hold a man in the unaccustomed posture, the external command "stop" is indispensable. A man cannot give the command "stop" to himself, for his will would not submit itself to this order. The reason for this lies in the fact that the combination of habitual postures, intellectual, emotional and moving, is stronger than the will. The command "stop," coming from outside, itself replaces the intellectual and emotional postures and, in this case, the moving posture submits itself to the will.

The three powers — economy

Man has three kinds of power. Each is independent in its nature, and each has its own laws and composition. But the sources of their formation are the same.

The first power is what is called physical power. Its quantity and quality depend on the structure and tissues of the human machine.

The second power is called psychic power. Its quality depends on a man's thinking center and the material it contains. What is called "will" and other similar things are functions of this power.

The third is called moral power. It depends on education and heredity.

The first two can easily be changed for they are easily formed. Moral power, on the other hand, is very hard to change, for it takes a long time to form.

If a man has common sense and sound logic, any action may change his opinion and his "will." But changing his nature, that is, his moral make-up, needs prolonged pressure.

All the three powers are material. Their quantity and quality depend on the quantity and quality of that which produces them. A man has more physical power if he has more muscles. For example, A. can lift more than B. The same applies to psychic power—it depends on the amount of material and data a man has.

In the same way, a man can have greater moral power if the conditions of his life have included influences of many ideas, religion and feeling. Thus, in order to change something, one must live a long time.

Moral and psychic power are also relative. It is often said, for instance, that man can change. But what he is, what he has been created by nature, he will remain. So, as in the case c physical strength, man cannot change; all he can do is to accı mulate force if he wants to increase. Of course if we are spea ing of a sick man, if he becomes healthy, he will be different.

Thus we see that the producer of energy cannot be changed; he will remain the same, but it is possible to increase the product. All three powers can be increased by economy and by right expenditure. If we learn this, it will be an achievement.

So a man can increase all three powers if he learns to practice economy and right expenditure. To economize and to know the proper way of spending energy makes a man a hundred times stronger than an athlete. If J. knew how to save and how to spend, she would at a given moment be a hundred times stronger than K., even physically. It is so in everything. Economy can be practiced also in psychic and moral matters.

Now let us examine physical power. For instance, in spite of the fact that you use different words and speak of different things than before, not one of you knows how to work. Not only do you spend much force unnecessarily when you work, but even when you do nothing. You can economize not only when you sit but also when you work. You can work five times harder and spend ten times less energy. For instance, when B. uses a hammer, he hammers with his whole body. If, for example, he spends ten pounds of force, then one pound is spent on the hammer and nine pounds quite unnecessarily. But to produce better results the hammer requires two pounds, and B.

gives it only half that amount. Instead of five minutes he takes ten; instead of one pound, he burns two pounds of coal. So he does not work as he should.

Sit as I sit, close your fists and take care to tighten your muscles only in your fists, as hard as you can. You see, everyone does it differently. One has tightened his legs, another his back.

If you pay attention, you will do it differently from the way you do ordinarily. Learn—when you sit, when you stand, when you lie down—to tense your right arm or your left. (*Speaking to M.*) Get up, tense your arm and keep the rest of your body relaxed. Try it in practice to understand better. When you pull, try to distinguish strain from resistance.

I now walk without tension, taking care only to keep my balance. If I stand still, I shall rock. Now I want to walk without spending any force. I only give an initial push, the rest goes by momentum. In this way I cross the room without having wasted any force. To do this you must let the movement do itself; it does not depend on you. I said earlier to someone that if he regulates his speed it shows that he is tensing his muscles.

Try to relax everything except your legs, and walk. Pay particular attention to keeping your body passive, but the head and face must be alive. The tongue and eyes must speak.

All day long, at every step, we are annoyed at something, like something, hate something, and so on. Now we are consciously relaxing some parts of our body and consciously tensing others. As we practice it, we do so with enjoyment. Each of us is able to do it more or less, and each one is sure that the more he practices it, the better he will be able to do it. All you need is practice; you must only want to and do it. The desire brings the possibility. I am speaking of physical things.

From tomorrow on, let each person also begin to practice the following exercise: if you are touched to the quick, see that it does not spread all over the body. Control your reaction; do not let it spread.

For instance, I have a problem: someone has insulted me. I don't want to forgive him, but I try to prevent the insult from affecting the whole of me. I dislike P.'s face. As soon as I see her, I have a feeling of antipathy. So I try not to be taken by this feeling. The point is not in the people—the point is the problem.

Now another thing. If everyone were nice and pleasant, I would have no opportunity for practical training; so I should be glad to have people to practice on.

Everything that touches us does so without our presence. It is arranged that way in us. We are slaves of it. For instance, she is antipathetic to me but she may be sympathetic to someone else. My reaction is in me. The thing that makes her antipathetic is in me. She is not to blame, she is antipathetic relative to myself. Everything that reaches us in the course of the day, and in the course of our whole life, is relative to us. At times what reaches us may be good.

This relativity is mechanical, just as the tensions in our muscles are mechanical. We are now learning to work. At the same time we also want to learn to be touched by what ought to touch us. As a rule we are touched by what ought not to touch us, for the things that touch us to the quick all day long should not have the power to touch us, since they have no real existence. This is an exercise in moral power.

And as regards psychic power, the thing to do is not to let "it" think, but to try to stop "it" often and often, whether what "it" thinks is good or bad. As soon as we remember, as soon as we catch ourselves, we must stop "it" from thinking.

In any case, such thinking will not discover an America, either in something good or something bad. Just as it is difficult at this moment not to tense your leg, so it is difficult not to let "it" think. But it is possible.

About the exercises. When you have practiced them, let those who have done them come to me for further ones. Now you have enough exercises for the present.

You must work with as few parts of the body as possible.

The principle of your work should be: to try to concentrate all the force you can on the parts of your body that are doing the work at the expense of the other parts.

Experiments with breathing

Can experimenting with breathing be useful?

All Europe has gone mad about breathing exercises. For four or five years I have made money by treating people who had ruined their breathing by such methods! Many books are written about it, everyone tries to teach others. They say: "The more you breathe, the greater the inflow of oxygen," etc., and, as a result, they come to me. I am very grateful to the authors of such books, founders of schools, and so on.

As you know, air is the second kind of food. Correct proportions are required in all things, in phenomena studied in chemistry, physics and so on. Crystallization can take place only with a certain correspondence, only then can something new be achieved.

Every matter has a certain density of vibrations. Interaction between matters can take place only with an exact correspondence between the vibrations of different matters. I have spoken of the Law of Three. For instance, if vibrations of positive matter are 300 and those of negative matter 100, combination is possible. Otherwise, if in practice vibrations do not correspond exactly to these figures, no combination will result; it will be a mechanical mixture which could be again resolved into its original component parts. It is not yet new matter.

[164]

The quantity of substances to be combined should also be in a certain definite proportion. You know that to obtain dough you need a definite amount of water for the amount of flour you want to use. If you take less water than is required, you will not have dough.

Your ordinary breathing is mechanical, and mechanically you take in as much air as you need. If there is more air it cannot combine in the way it should; so a right proportion is necessary.

If artificially controlled breathing is practiced as it usually is, it results in disharmony. Therefore, in order to escape the harm which artificial breathing may bring, one must correspondingly change the other foods. And this is possible only with full knowledge. For instance, the stomach needs a definite quantity of food, not only for nutrition but because it is accustomed to it. We eat more than we need simply for taste, simply for satisfaction, and because the stomach is used to a certain pressure. You know that the stomach has certain nerves. When there is no pressure in the stomach, these nerves stimulate the stomach muscles and we have a sensation of hunger.

Many organs work mechanically, without our conscious participation. Each of them has its own rhythm, and the rhythms of different organs stand in a definite relationship to one another.

If, for example, we change our breathing, we change the rhythm of our lungs; but since everything is connected, other rhythms also gradually begin to change. If we go on with this breathing for a long time it may change the rhythm of all the organs. For instance, the rhythm of the stomach will change. And the stomach has its own habits, it needs a certain time to digest food; say, for example, the food must lie there an hour. If the rhythm of the stomach changes, food may pass through more quickly and the stomach will not have time to take from it all it needs. In another place the reverse may occur.

It is a thousand times better not to interfere with our machine, to leave it in bad condition rather than correct it without knowledge. For the human organism is a very complicated apparatus containing many organs with different rhythms and different requirements, and many organs are connected with one another. Either everything must be changed or nothing, otherwise instead of good one may do harm. Artificial breathing is the cause of many illnesses. Only accidentally, in isolated cases where a man manages to stop in time, does he avoid harming himself. If a man practices it long, the results are always bad.

To work on oneself one must know every screw, every nail of one's machine—then you will know what to do. But if you know a little and try, you may lose a great deal. The risk is great, for the machine is very complicated. It has very small screws which can be easily damaged, and if you push harder you may break them. And these screws cannot be bought in a shop.

One must be very careful. When you know, it is another thing. If anyone here is experimenting with breathing, it is better to stop while there is still time.

First talk in Berlin

You ask about the aim of the movements. To each position of the body corresponds a certain inner state and, on the other hand, to each inner state corresponds a certain posture. A man, in his life, has a certain number of habitual postures and he passes from one to another without stopping at those between.

Taking new, unaccustomed postures enables you to observe yourself inside differently from the way you usually do in ordinary conditions. This becomes especially clear when on the command "Stop!" you have to freeze at once. At this command you have to freeze not only externally but also to stop all your inner movements. Muscles that were tense must remain in the same state of tension, and the muscles that were relaxed must remain relaxed. You must make the effort to keep thoughts and feelings as they were, and at the same time to observe yourself.

For instance, you wish to become an actress. Your habitual postures are suited to acting a certain part—for instance, a maid—yet you have to act the part of a countess. A countess has quite different postures. In a good dramatic school you would be taught, say, two hundred postures. For a countess the characteristic postures are, say, postures number 14, 68,

101 and 142. If you know this, when you are on the stage you
have simply to pass from one posture to another, and then
however badly you may act you will be a countess all the time.
But if you don't know these postures, then even a person who
has quite an untrained eye will feel that you are not a countess
but a maid.

It is necessary to observe yourself differently than you do in
ordinary life. It is necessary to have a different attitude, not
the attitude you had till now. You know where your habitual
attitudes have led you till now. There is no sense in going on
as before, either for you or for me, for I have no desire to work
with you if you remain as you are. You want knowledge, but
what you have had until today was not knowledge. It was only
mechanical collecting of information. It is knowledge not in
you but outside you. It has no value. What concern is it of
yours that what you know was created at one time by somebody else? You have not created it, therefore it is of small
value. You say, for instance, that you know how to set type for
newspapers, and you value this in yourself. But now a machine
can do that. Combining is not creating.

Everyone has a limited repertoire of habitual postures, and
of inner states. She is a painter and you will say, perhaps, that
she has her own style. But it is not style, it is limitation. Whatever her pictures may represent, they will always be the same,
whether she paints a picture of European life or of the East. I
will at once recognize that she, and nobody else, has painted
it. An actor who is the same in all his roles—just himself—what
kind of an actor is he? Only by accident can he have a role
that entirely corresponds to what he is in life.

In general, until today all knowledge has been mechanical
as everything else has been mechanical. For example, I look at
her with kindliness; she at once becomes kindly. If I look at
her angrily, she is at once displeased—and not only with me
but with her neighbor, and this neighbor with someone else,
and so it goes on. She is angry because I have looked at her
crossly. She is angry mechanically. But to become angry of her

own free will, she cannot. She is a slave to the attitudes of others. And it would not be so bad if all these others were always living beings, but she is also a slave to all things. Any object is stronger than she. It is continuous slavery. Your functions are not yours, but you yourself are the function of what goes on in you.

To new things one must learn to have new attitudes. You see, now everybody is listening in his own way, but a way corresponding to his inner posture. For example, "*Starosta*" listens with his mind, and you with your feeling; and if all of you were asked to repeat, everyone would repeat in his own way in accordance with his inner state of the moment. One hour passes, someone tells something unpleasant to "*Starosta*," while you are given a mathematical problem to solve. "*Starosta*" will repeat what he heard here colored by his feeling, and you will do it in a logical form.

And all this is because only one center is working—for instance, either mind or feeling. Yet you must learn to listen in a new way. The knowledge you have had up to today is the knowledge of one center—knowledge without understanding. Are there many things you know and at the same time understand? For instance, you know what electricity is, but do you understand it as clearly as you understand that twice two makes four? The latter you understand so clearly that no one can prove to you the contrary; but with electricity it is different. Today it is explained to you in one way—you believe it. Tomorrow you will be given a different explanation—you will also believe that. But understanding is perception not by one but by not less than two centers. There exists a more complete perception, but for the moment it is enough if you make one center control the other. If one center perceives and the other approves the perception, agrees with it or rejects it, this is understanding. If an argument between centers fails to produce a definite result, it will be half-understanding. Half-understanding is also no good. It is necessary that everything you listen to here, everything you talk about among yourselves elsewhere, should be said or listened to not with one center but with two. Otherwise there will be no right result either for me or for you. For you it will be as before, a mere accumulation of new information.

All exercises that may be given in the Institute can be divided into seven categories. The center of gravity of the first category is that they are specially for the body. The second kind, specially for the mind. The third kind, specially for the feeling. The fourth kind, mind and body together. The fifth kind, for body and feeling. The sixth kind, for feelings, thoughts and body. The seventh kind, for all three together and our automatism. It must be noted that we live most of all in this automatism. If we lived the whole time by centers alone they would not have enough energy. Therefore this automatism is quite indispensable to us, although at the present moment it is our greatest enemy from which we have temporarily to free ourselves in order, first, to form a conscious body and mind. Later, this automatism must be studied for the purpose of adapting it.

Until we are free of automatism, we cannot learn anything else. We must do away with it temporarily.

Certain exercises are already known to us. For example, we study exercises for the body. The various tasks we have done were elementary exercises for the mind. We have not yet done any exercises for the feelings—these are more complex. At first they are even difficult to visualize. Yet they are of the foremost importance to us. The realm of feeling comes first in our inner life; indeed all our misfortunes are due to disorganized feeling. We have too much material of that kind and we live on it the whole time.

But at the same time we have no feeling. I mean that we have neither objective nor subjective feeling. The whole realm of our feeling is filled with something alien and completely mechanical. There are three kinds of feeling—subjective, objective and automatic. For example, there is no feeling of morality either subjective or objective.

The objective feeling of morality is connected with certain general, orderly and immutable moral laws, established over the centuries, in accordance both chemically and physically with human circumstances and nature, established objectively for all and connected with nature (or, as is said, with God).

The subjective feeling of morality is when a man, on the basis of his own experience and his own personal qualities, his personal observations, a sense of justice entirely his own, and so on, forms a personal conception of morality, on the basis of which he lives.

Both the first and the second feeling of morality are not only absent in people but people even have no idea of them.

What we say about morality relates to everything.

We have in our minds a more or less theoretical idea of morality. We have heard and we have read. But we cannot apply it to life. We live as our mechanism allows us. Theoretically we know that we should love N., but in actual fact he may be antipathetic to us—we may not like his nose. I understand with my mind that emotionally also I should have a right attitude to him, but I am unable to. Somewhere far away from N., I can in the course of a year decide to have a good attitude toward him. But if certain mechanical associations have established themselves, it will be just the same as before when I see him again. With us the feeling of morality is automatic. I may have established a rule for myself to think in this way, but "it" does not live like that.

If we wish to work on ourselves we must not be only subjective; we must accustom ourselves to understand what objective means. Subjective feeling cannot be the same in everyone, since all people are different. One is English, another a Jew; one likes plover, and so on. We are all different, but our differences should be united by objective laws. In certain circumstances small subjective laws are sufficient. But in communal life justice can be attained only through the objective. Objective laws are very limited. If all people had this small number of laws in them, our inner and outer life would be a great deal happier. There would be no loneliness, nor would there be unhappy states.

From the most ancient times through experience of life and wise statesmanship, life itself gradually evolved fifteen commandments and established them for the good of individuals as well as for all peoples. If these fifteen commandments were actually in us all, we would be able to understand, to love, to hate. We would have levers for the basis of right judgment.

All religions, all teachings come from God and speak in the name of God. This does not mean that God actually gave them, but they are connected with one whole and with what we call God.

For example: God said, Love thy parents and thou wilt love me. And indeed, whoever does not love his parents cannot love God.

Before we go any further, let us pause and ask ourselves: Did we love our parents, did we love them as they deserved, or was it simply a case of "it loves," and how should we have loved?

As it is with everything, so it is with movements. Movements are performed without the participation of other parts of the organism. Such movements are harmful for the organism. It is useful for its consequences. I emphasize for its consequences. But, for the particular scale to which the organism is accustomed, every movement which exceeds this scale is harmful at first, for a short time. Movements become useful in the future if they are accompanied by proper calculations.

Movements, taken as work, can be divided into the following categories:

1) When one takes the peculiarities of a man's constitution into consideration, both those present now and those which may be likely in the future.
2) When breathing participates in movement.
3) When thought participates in movement.
4) When a man's old, constant, unchangingly characteristic movement takes part.

Only if movements are connected with the things which I have enumerated can they be useful for ordinary, everyday life.

I separate the idea of everyday life from the idea of life connected with work for self-perfection and inner development. By everyday life, I mean a normal, healthy life.

[174]

For our work, apart from the four categories I have enumerated, we have to join our normal feelings and sensations with movement, as well as the special feeling and special sensation which we are aiming to acquire. This other sensation should be acquired without destroying the sensations already present.

So there are four conditions.

Thus you see that to make a movement truly useful we must gradually join with it all the above-mentioned other movements of a different category. You must realize that only then can a movement be useful. No result can be expected if even one of the conditions mentioned is lacking.

The easiest of our movements is that crude organic movement which we are able to do (which we have studied already). The movements we have been doing so far are those that all people do, and everyone can do them. And although the movements we shall be doing may look complicated at the first glance, they can easily be done by everyone if they are sufficiently practiced.

However, if we begin to add to these movements one of the conditions I mentioned, it will prove much more difficult and will no longer be possible for everyone. And if we gradually add to it several conditions, such a movement will become possible for only a very limited number of people.

In the end, in order to make a beginning in achieving the aim for the sake of which we began to study movements, it is necessary gradually to join to the movement which proceeds in us the conditions I spoke about.

Now, to begin with, it is essential to pick out the more or less appropriate types. Together with this we shall gradually study and practice the second condition—that is, breathing.

At first we shall be divided into groups; later we shall divide groups themselves, and in this way shall come to individuals.

The actor

Question: Is the actor's profession useful in developing coordinated work of centers?

Answer: The more an actor acts, the more the work of centers becomes separated in him. In order to act, one must first of all be an artist.

We have spoken about the spectrum producing white light. A man can be called an actor only if he is able, so to speak, to produce a white light. A real actor is one who creates, one who can produce all the seven colors of the spectrum. There have been and are even today such artists. But in modern times an actor is generally only outwardly an actor.

Like any other man, an actor has a definite number of basic postures; his other postures are only different combinations of these. All roles are built out of postures. It is impossible to acquire new postures by practice; practice can only strengthen old ones. The longer you go on, the more difficult it becomes to learn new postures—the fewer possibilities there are.

All the intensity of the actor is in vain: it is only a waste of energy. If this material were saved and spent on something new, it would be more useful. As it is, it is spent on old things.

[176]

Only in his own and other people's imagination does an actor appear to create. In actual fact, he cannot create.

In our work, this profession cannot help; on the contrary, it spoils things for tomorrow. The sooner a man abandons this occupation, the better for tomorrow, the easier it is to start something new.

Talent can be made in twenty-four hours. Genius exists, but an ordinary man cannot be a genius. It is only a word.

It is the same in all the arts. Real art cannot be the work of an ordinary man. He cannot act, he cannot be "I." An actor cannot have what another man has—he cannot feel as another man feels. If he plays the part of a priest, he ought to have the understanding and feelings of a priest. But he can have these only if he has all the priest's material, all that a priest knows and understands. And it is so with every profession; special knowledge is required. The artist without knowledge only imagines.

Associations work in a definite way in each person. I see a man making a certain movement. This gives me a shock, and from this associations start. A policeman would probably assume that the man wanted to pick my pocket. But supposing the man never thought of my pocket, I, as the policeman, would not have understood the movement. If I am a priest, I have other associations; I think the movement has something to do with the soul, though the man is actually thinking of my pocket.

Only if I know the psychology both of the priest and of the policeman, and their different approaches, can I understand with my mind; only if I have corresponding feelings and postures in my body can I know with my mind what will be their thinking associations, and also which thinking associations evoke in them which feeling associations. This is the first point.

Knowing the machine, I give orders every moment for associations to change—but I have to do this at every moment. Every moment associations change automatically, one evokes another and so on. If I am acting, I have to direct at every moment. It is impossible to leave it to momentum. And I can direct only if there is someone present who is able to direct.

My thought cannot direct—it is occupied. My feelings are also occupied. So there must be someone there who is not engaged in acting, not engaged in life—only then is it possible to direct.

A man who has "I" and who knows what is required in every respect can act. A man who has no "I" cannot act.

An ordinary actor cannot play a role—his associations are different. He may have the appropriate costume and keep approximately to suitable postures, make grimaces as the producer or the author directs. The author must also know all this.

In order to be a real actor, one must be a real man. A real man can be an actor and a real actor can be a man.

Everyone should try to be an actor. This is a high aim. The aim of every religion, of every knowledge, is to be an actor. But at present all are actors.

Creative art — associations

Question: Is it necessary to study the mathematical foundations of art, or can works of art be created without such a study?

Answer: Without this study, one can expect only accidental results; repetition cannot be expected.

Question: Can there be no unconscious creative art, coming from feeling?

Answer: There can be no unconscious creative art, and our feeling is very stupid. It sees only one side, whereas understanding of everything must be of all sides. Studying history we see that there were such accidental results, but it is not a rule.

Question: Can one write music harmonically, without knowledge of mathematical laws?

Answer: There will be harmony between one note and another and there will be chords, but there will be no harmony among the harmonies. We are speaking now of influence, of conscious influence. A composer can exert an influence.

[179]

As things are at present, anything can bring a man into one or another state. Supposing you feel happy. At this moment there is a noise, a bell, some music—any tune, it may be a fox-trot. You forget entirely that you have heard it, but later, when you hear the same music, or the same bell, it evokes the same feeling by association: let us say, love. This too is an influence, but it is subjective. Not only music but any kind of noise may serve as association here. If it is connected with something unpleasant, as, for instance, with having lost some money, an unpleasant association will result.

But we are speaking of objective art, of objective laws in music or in painting.

The art we know is subjective, for without mathematical knowledge there can be no objective art. Accidental results are very rare.

Associations are a very powerful and important phenomenon for us, but their significance is already forgotten. In ancient times people had special feast days. One day, for instance, was dedicated to certain combinations of sound, another to flowers, or colors, a third to taste, another to the weather, coldness and heat. Then the different sensations were compared.

For example, supposing one day was the feast of sound. One hour there would be one sound, another hour another sound. During this time a special drink was handed around, or at times a special "smoke." In a word, certain states and feelings were evoked by chemical means with the help of external influences, in order to create certain associations for the future. Later when similar external circumstances were repeated, they evoked the same states.

There was even a special day for mice, snakes and animals we are generally afraid of. People were given a special drink and then made to handle such things as snakes in order to get used to them. This produced such an impression that afterwards a man was not afraid any more. Such customs existed a long time ago in Persia and Armenia. In former times people understood human psychology very well and were guided by it. But the reasons were never explained to the masses; they were given quite a different interpretation, from a different angle. Only the priests knew the meaning of it all. These facts refer to the pre-Christian times when people were ruled by priest-kings.

Question: Do dances only serve to control the body or have they also a mystical significance?

Answer: Dances are for the mind. They give nothing to the soul—the soul does not need anything. A dance has a certain meaning; every movement has a certain content.

But the soul does not drink whiskey, it does not like it. It likes another food which it receives independently of us.

Questions and answers on art, etc.

Question: Does the work of the Institute necessitate giving up our own work for some years, or can it be carried on at the same time?

Answer: Institute work is inner work; so far you only do outer work, but this is quite different. For some it may be necessary to stop outer work, for others not.

Question: Is the aim to develop and reach a balance, so that we may become stronger than the outside and develop into superman?

Answer: Man must realize that he cannot do. All our activities are set in motion by external impetus; it is all mechanical. You cannot do even if you wish to do.

Question: What place do art and creative work occupy in your teaching?

Answer: Present-day art is not necessarily creative. But for us art is not an aim but a means.

Ancient art has a certain inner content. In the past, art served the same purpose as is served today by books—the pur-

pose of preserving and transmitting certain knowledge. In ancient times they did not write books but expressed knowledge
in works of art. We shall find many ideas in the ancient art
which has reached us, if we know how to read it. Every art
was like that then, including music. And people of ancient
times looked on art in this way.

You saw our movements and dances. But all you saw was
the outer form—beauty, technique. But I do not like the external side you see. For me, art is a means for harmonious development. In everything we do the underlying idea is to do
what cannot be done automatically and without thought.

Ordinary gymnastics and dances are mechanical. If our aim
is a harmonious development of man, then for us, dances and
movements are a means of combining the mind and the feeling
with movements of the body and manifesting them together.
In all things, we have the aim to develop something which
cannot be developed directly or mechanically—which inter-
prets the whole man: mind, body and feeling.

The second purpose of dances is study. Certain movements
carry a proof in them, a definite knowledge, or religious and
philosophical ideas. In some of them one can even read a rec-
ipe for cooking some dish.

In many parts of the East the inner content of one or another dance is now almost forgotten, yet people continue to
dance it simply from habit.

Thus movements have two aims: study and development.

Question: Does this mean that all Western art has no significance?

Answer: I studied Western art after studying the ancient art
of the East. To tell you the truth, I found nothing in the West
to compare with Eastern art. Western art has much that is external, sometimes a great deal of philosophy; but Eastern art is
precise, mathematical, without manipulations. It is a form of
script.

Question: Haven't you found something similar in the ancient art of the West?

Answer: In studying history we see how everything gradually changes. It is the same with religious ceremonies. At first they had meaning and those who performed them understood this meaning. But little by little the meaning was forgotten and ceremonies continued to be performed mechanically. It is the same with art.

For example, to understand a book written in English, it is necessary to know English. I am not speaking of fantasy but of mathematical, non-subjective art. A modern painter may believe in and feel his art, but you see it subjectively: one person likes it, another dislikes it. It is a case of feeling, of like and dislike.

But ancient art was not for liking. Everyone who read understood. Now, this purpose of art is entirely forgotten.

For instance, take architecture. I saw some examples of architecture in Persia and Turkey—for instance, one building of two rooms. Everyone who entered these rooms, whether old or young, whether English or Persian, wept. This happened with people of different backgrounds and education. We continued this experiment for two or three weeks and observed everyone's reactions. The result was always the same. We specially chose cheerful people. With these architectural combinations, the mathematically calculated vibrations contained in the building could not produce any other effect. We are under certain laws and cannot withstand external influences. Because the architect of this building had a different understanding and built mathematically, the result was always the same.

We made another experiment. We tuned our musical instruments in a special way and so combined the sounds that even by bringing in casual passersby from the street we obtained the result we wanted. The only difference was that one felt more, another less.

You come to a monastery. You are not a religious man, but

what is played and sung there evokes in you a desire to pray. Later you will be surprised by this. And so it is with everyone.

This objective art is based on laws, whereas modern music is entirely subjective. It is possible to prove where everything in this subjective art comes from.

Question: Is mathematics the basis of all art?

Answer: All Eastern ancient art.

Question: Then could anyone who knew the formula build a perfect form like a cathedral, producing the same emotion?

Answer: Yes, and get the same reactions, too.

Question: Then art is knowledge, not talent?

Answer: It is knowledge. Talent is relative. I could teach you to sing well in a week, even without a voice.

Question: So if I knew mathematics, I could write like Schubert?

Answer: Knowledge is necessary—mathematics and physics.

Question: Occult physics?

Answer: All knowledge is one. If you only know the four rules of arithmetic, then decimal fractions are higher mathematics for you.

Question: To write music, wouldn't you need an idea as well as knowledge?

Answer: The mathematical law is the same for everyone. All mathematically constructed music is the result of movements.

At one time I conceived the idea of observing movements, so while traveling and collecting material about art I observed only movements. Coming back home, I played music in accordance with the movements I had observed and it proved identical with the actual music, for the man who wrote it wrote mathematically. Yet while observing the movements I did not listen to the music, for I had no time.

(*Someone asks a question about the tempered scale.*)

Answer: In the East they have the same octave as we have—from do to do. Only here we divide the octave into 7, while there they have different divisions: into 48, 7, 4, 23, 30. But the law is the same everywhere: from do to do, the same octave.

Each note also contains seven. The finer the ear, the greater the number of divisions.

In the Institute we use quarter tones because Western instruments have no smaller divisions. With the piano one has to make a certain compromise, but stringed instruments allow the use of quarter tones. In the East they not only use quarters but a seventh of a tone.

To foreigners, Eastern music seems monotonous, they only wonder at its crudity and musical poverty. But what sounds like one note to them is a whole melody for the local inhabitants—a melody contained in one note. This kind of melody is much more difficult than ours. If an Eastern musician makes a mistake in his melody the result is cacophony for them, but for a European the whole thing is a rhythmic monotone. In this respect, only a man who grew up there can distinguish good and bad music.

Question: Given mathematical knowledge, would a man express himself in one of the arts?

Answer: For development there is no limit, for young or old.

Question: In what direction?

Answer: In all directions.

Question: Do we need to wish for it?

Answer: It is not merely wishing. First I will explain about development. There is the law of evolution and involution. Everything is in motion, both organic life and inorganic, either up or down. But evolution has its limits, as well as involution. As an example, let us take the musical scale of seven notes. From one do to the other there is one place where there is a stop. When you touch the keys, you start a do—a vibration which has a certain momentum in it. With its vibration it can go a certain distance till it starts another note vibrating, namely re, then mi. Up to that point the notes have an inner possibility of going on, but here, if there is no outside push, the octave goes back. If it gets this outside help, it can go on by itself for a long way. Man is also constructed in accordance with this law.

Man serves as an apparatus in the development of this law. I eat, but Nature has made me for a certain purpose, I must evolve. I do not eat for myself but for some outside purpose. I eat because this thing cannot evolve by itself without my help. I eat some bread, I also take in air and impressions. These come in from outside and then work by law. It is the law of the octave. If we take any note, it can become a do. Do contains both possibility and momentum; it can rise to re and mi without help. Bread can evolve, but if not mixed with air it cannot become fa: this energy helps it to pass a difficult place. After that it needs no help until si, but it can go no further than this by itself. Our aim is to help the octave to completion. Si is the highest point in ordinary animal life, and it is the matter from which a new body can be built.

Question: Is the soul separate?

Answer: All law is one; but the soul is remote, while just now we are talking of nearby things. But this law, the law of the trinity, is everywhere—there can be no new thing without the third force.

Question: Can you get past the stop by means of the third force?

Answer: Yes, if you have knowledge. Nature arranged it so that air and bread are chemically quite different, and cannot mix; but as bread changes in re and mi, it becomes more permeable, so that they can mix.

Now you must work on yourself, you are do; when you get to mi, you can meet help.

Question: By accident?

Answer: One piece of bread I eat, another I throw away; is this accident? Man is a factory with three stories. There are three doors by which the raw materials are taken in to their respective storage rooms where they are stored. If it were a sausage factory, the world would only see carcasses taken in and sausages coming out. But in actual fact it is a much more complicated arrangement. If we wish to build a factory like the one we are studying, we must first look at all the machines and inspect them in detail. The law "as above, so below" is the same everywhere; it is all one law. We also have in us the sun, the moon, and the planets, only on a very small scale.

Everything is in movement, everything has emanations, because everything eats something and is itself eaten by something. The earth also has emanations, and so has the sun, and these emanations are matter. The earth has an atmosphere which limits its emanations. Between the earth and the sun there are three kinds of emanations; the emanations of the earth go only a short distance, those of the planets go much further, but not all the way to the sun. Between us and the sun there are three kinds of matter, each with a different density. First—the matter near the earth, containing its emanations; then the matter containing emanations of the planets; and still further—the matter where there are only emanations of the sun. The densities stand in the ratio 1, 2, and 4, and vibrations are in an inverse ratio, as finer matter has a greater rate of vibration. But beyond our sun are other suns which also have emanations and send influences and matter, and beyond them there is the source, which we can only express mathematically, also with its emanations. These higher places are beyond the reach of the sun's emanations.

If we take the material from the uttermost limit as 1, then the more divisions of matter according to density, the higher the numbers. The same law goes through everything, the Law of Three—positive, negative, neutralizing. When the first two forces are mixed with a third, something quite different is created. For example, flour and water remain flour and water—there is no change; but if you add fire, then fire will bake them and a new thing will be created which has different properties.

Unity consists of three matters. In religion we have a prayer: God the Father, God the Son and God the Holy Ghost, Three in One—expressing the law rather than a fact. This fundamental unity is used in physics, and taken as the standard of unity. The three matters are "carbon," "oxygen" and "nitrogen," and together they make the "hydrogen" which is the foundation of all matter, whatever its density. The Cosmos is an octave of seven notes, each note of which can be subdivided into a further octave, and again and again to the uttermost divisible atom. Everything is arranged in octaves, each octave being one note of a greater octave, until you come to the Cosmic Octave. From the Absolute, emanations go in every direction, but we will take one—the Cosmic Ray on which we are: the Moon, Organic Life, the Earth, the Planets, the Sun, All Suns, the Absolute. The Cosmic Ray goes no further.

Emanations from the Absolute meet other matter and are

converted into new matter, gradually becoming denser and denser and changing according to law. We can take these emanations from the Absolute as threefold, but when mixed with the next order of matter they become six. And since, as in ourselves, there is both evolution and involution, the process can go either up or down, and do has the power to transform into si, or in the other direction into re. The octave of the Earth needs help at mi, which it gets from the Planets, to turn mi into fa.

Question: Based on the octave, is it possible to conceive of other cosmoses with a different arrangement?

Answer: This law is all-prevailing, it has been proved by experiments.

Question: Man has an octave inside him; but what about higher possibilities?

Answer: This is the aim of all religions, to find out how to do. It cannot be done unconsciously, but is taught by a system.

Question: Is it a gradual unfolding?

Answer: Up to a certain limit, but later there comes the difficult place (mi-fa) and it is necessary to find how to pass to it in accordance with law.

Question: Is the limit the same for everyone?

Answer: The ways of approach are different, but all must get to "Philadelphia." The limits are the same.

Question: With mathematical law could everyone be developed to a higher degree?

Answer: The body, when born, is the result of many things, and is just an empty possibility. Man is born without a soul, but it is possible to make one. Heredity is not important for the soul. Each man has many things he must change; they are individual; but, beyond that point, preparation cannot help.

The ways are different, but all must get to "Philadelphia"— this is the basic aim of all religions. But each goes by a special route. Special preparation is necessary; all our functions must be coordinated and all our parts developed. After "Philadelphia," the road is one.

Man is three persons with different languages, different desires, different development and upbringing; but later—all is the same. There is only one religion, for all must be equal in development.

You may start as a Christian, a Buddhist, a Moslem, and work along the line you are accustomed to, and start from one center. But afterwards the others must be developed too.

Sometimes religion deliberately hides things, for otherwise we could not work. In Christianity faith is an absolute necessity, and Christians must develop feeling; and for that it is necessary to work only on that function. If you believe, you can do all the necessary exercises. But without faith you could not do them productively.

If we want to cross the room, we may not be able to go straight across, for the way is very difficult. The teacher knows this and knows that we must go to the left, but does not tell us. Though going to the left is our subjective aim, our responsibility is to get across. Then, when we arrive there and are past the difficulty, we must have a new aim again. We are three, not one, each with different desires. Even if our mind knows how important the aim is, the horse cares for nothing but its food; so sometimes we must manipulate and fool the horse.

But whichever way we take, our aim is to develop our soul, to fulfil our higher destiny. We are born in one river where the

Views from the Real World

drops are passive, but he who works for himself is passive on the outside and active inside. Both lives are according to law: one goes by the way of involution and the other by evolution.

Question: Are you happy when you get to "Philadelphia"?

Answer: I only know two chairs. No chair is unhappy: here it is happy, and that other chair is also happy. Man can always look for a better chair. When he begins looking for a better one, it always means that he is disillusioned, because if he is satisfied, he does not look for another one. Sometimes his chair is so bad that he cannot sit on it any longer and decides that as it is so bad where he is, he will look for something else.

Question: What happens after "Philadelphia"?

Answer: A very small thing. At present it is very bad for the carriage that there are only passengers, all giving orders as they please—no permanent master. After "Philadelphia" there is a master in charge, who thinks for all, arranges everything and sees that things are right. I am sure it is clear that it is better for all to have a master.

Question: You advised sincerity. I have discovered that I would rather be a happy fool than an unhappy philosopher.

Answer: You believe you are not satisfied with yourself. I push you. You are quite mechanical, you cannot do anything, you are hallucinated. When you look with one center you are entirely under hallucination; when with two you are half-free; but if you look with three centers you cannot be under hallucination at all. You must begin by collecting material. You can have no bread without baking; knowledge is water, body is flour, and emotion—suffering—is fire.

IV

All this teaching given in fragments must be pieced together, and observations and actions must be connected to it. If there is no paste, nothing will stick.

(Prieuré, July 17, 1922 and March 2, 1923)

All our emotions are rudimentary organs of "something higher," e.g., fear may be an organ of future clairvoyance, anger of real force, etc.

(Prieuré, July 29, 1922)

The secret of being able to assimilate the involving part of air is to try to realize your true significance, and the true significance of those around you . . .

From looking at your neighbor and realizing his true significance, and that he will die, pity and compassion will arise in you for him and finally you will love him.

(New York, February 8, 1931)

If you help others, you will be helped, perhaps tomorrow, perhaps in 100 years, but you will be helped. Nature must pay off the debt. . . . It is a mathematical law and all life is mathematics.

(Prieuré, August 12, 1924)

Looking backwards, we only remember the difficult periods of our lives, never the peaceful times; the latter are sleep, the former are struggle and therefore life.

(Prieuré, August 12, 1924)

God the Word

At the beginning of every religion we find an affirmation of the existence of God the Word and the Word-God.

One teaching says that when the world was still nothing, there were emanations, there was God the Word. God the Word is the world. God said: "Let it be so," and sent the Father and the Son. He is always sending the Father and the Son. And once He sent the Holy Ghost.

Everything in the world obeys the Law of Three, everything existing came into being in accordance with this law. Combinations of positive and negative principles can produce new results, different from the first and the second, only if a third force comes in.

If I affirm, she denies and we argue. But nothing new is created until something else is added to the discussion. Then something new arises.

Take the Ray of Creation. At the top is the Absolute, God the Word, divided into three: God the Father, God the Son and God the Holy Ghost.

The Absolute creates in accordance with the same law. Only in this case all the three forces necessary to produce a new manifestation are in the Absolute Himself. He sends them forth from Himself, emanates them.

Sometimes the three forces change their places.

The three forces or principles, issuing from the Absolute, have created the whole multitude of suns, one of which is our sun. Everything has emanations. The interaction of emanations produces new combinations. This refers to man, to the earth and to the microbe. Each of the suns also emanates, and emanations of the suns, by means of combinations of positive and negative matter, give rise to new formations. The result of one of these combinations is our earth, and the newest combination is our moon.

After the act of creation, existence and emanations go on. Emanations penetrate everywhere according to their possibilities. Thus emanations also reach man.

The result of the interaction of emanations is new frictions.

The difference between the creative activity of the Absolute and subsequent acts of creation consists in the fact that, as I have said, the Absolute creates from Himself. Only the Absolute has Will; He alone sends forth the three forces from Himself. Subsequent acts of creation proceed mechanically, by means of interaction based on the same Law of Three. No single entity can create by itself—only collective creation is possible.

The direction of the creative activity of the Absolute proceeding toward man is the direction of momentum. According to the Law of Seven, development can go on only as far as a certain point.

We have taken the line issuing from the Absolute and passing through us. This line, able to proceed only as far as a certain point, ends in our moon. The moon is the last point of creation on this line.

The result is something like a ladder, and the moon is the base of this ladder. The main points of this line of creation are: Absolute, Sun, Earth, and the last point, Moon. Between these four points there are three octaves: Absolute—Sun; Sun—Earth; Earth—Moon. Each of these points is a do. Between them, at three points, there are, as it were, three machines whose function is to make fa pass into mi.

All through the cosmic octave the shock at fa must come from outside, and the shock at si comes from inside the do. By means of these, involution proceeds from top to bottom and evolution from bottom to top. The life of man plays the same role as planets in relation to earth, earth in relation to moon and all suns in relation to our sun.

The matter which comes from the Absolute is hydrogen, resulting from a combination of carbon, oxygen and nitrogen. One hydrogen combining with another turns it into another kind of hydrogen with its own qualities and density.

Everything is governed by law—which is very simple. I have shown you how the law works outside; now you can find out how it works in you. In accordance with the law, you can follow either the law of evolution or the law of involution. You must put the outside law inside.

In our system we are similar to God—threefold. If we consciously receive three matters and send them out, we can construct outside what we like. This is creation. When they are received through us it is the creation of the creator. In this case, all three forces manifest through us and blend outside. Every creation can be either subjective or objective.

Question: What is the neutralizing element in the birth of man?

Answer: Some kind of color mixed with the active and passive principles; it too is material and has special vibrations. All the planets project their vibrations on the earth, and all life is colored by the vibrations of the planet nearest to the earth at a given moment. All planets have emanations, and the emanations of each particular planet are strongest when it is nearest to the earth. Planets project special influences, but each special influence stays unmixed only for a short time. Sometimes the totality has special vibrations. Here, too, the three principles must correspond to one another in accordance with law; when their relationship is correct there can be crystallization.

(Question about the moon)

Answer: The moon is man's big enemy. We serve the moon. Last time you heard about kundabuffer. Kundabuffer is the moon's representative on earth. We are like the moon's sheep, which it cleans, feeds and shears, and keeps for its own purposes. But when it is hungry it kills a lot of them. All organic life works for the moon. Passive man serves involution; and active man, evolution. You must choose. But there is a principle: in one service you can hope for a career; in the other you receive much but without a career. In both cases we are slaves, for in both cases we have a master. Inside us we also have a moon, a sun and so on. We are a whole system. If you know what your moon is and does, you can understand the cosmos.

Everywhere and always there is affirmation and negation, not only in individuals but in the whole of mankind as well. If one half of mankind affirms something, the other half denies it. For instance, there are two opposing currents—science and religion. What science affirms, religion denies and vice versa. This is a mechanical law and it cannot be otherwise. It operates everywhere and on every scale—in the world, in cities, in the family, in the inner life of an individual man. One center of a man affirms, another denies. We are always a particle of these two.

It is an objective law and everybody is a slave of this law; for instance, I must be a slave of either science or religion. In either case man is a slave of this objective law. It is impossible to free oneself from it. Only he is free who stands in the middle. If he can do this, he escapes from this general law of slavery. But how to escape? It is very difficult. We are not strong enough not to submit to this law. We are slaves. We are weak. Yet the possibility exists of our getting free from this law; if we try slowly, gradually, but steadily. From the objective point of view this means, of course, to go against the law, against nature, in other words, to commit sin. But we can do so because a law of a different order exists as well; we have been given another law by God.

What then is necessary to achieve this? Let us take again the first example: religion and science. I shall discuss this with myself, and each man should try to do the same.

I reason in this way: I am a small man. I have only lived for fifty years, and religion has existed for thousands of years. Thousands of men have studied these religions and yet I deny them. I ask myself: "Is it possible that they were all fools and that only I am clever?" The situation is the same with science. It has also existed for many years. Suppose I deny it. Again the same question arises: "Can it be that I alone am more clever than all the multitude of men who have studied science for so long a time?"

If I reason impartially I shall understand that I may be more intelligent than one or two men but not than a thousand. If I am a normal man and I reason without being biased, I shall understand that I cannot be more intelligent than millions. I repeat, I am but a small man. How can I criticize religion and science? What then is possible? I begin to think that perhaps there is some truth in them; it is impossible for everyone to be mistaken. So now I set myself the task of trying to understand what it is all about. When I begin to think and study impartially, I find that religion and science are both right, in spite of the fact that they are opposed to one another. I discover a small mistake. One side takes one subject; the other side, another. Or they study the same subject but from different angles; or one studies the causes, the other the effects of the same phenomenon, and so they never meet. But both are right, for both are based on laws that are mathematically exact. If we take only the result, we shall never understand in what the difference consists.

Question: In what way does your system differ from the philosophy of the yogis?

Answer: Yogis are idealists; we are materialists. I am a skeptic. The first injunction inscribed on the walls of the Institute is: "Believe nothing, not even yourself." I believe only if I have statistical proof; that is, only if I have obtained the same result over and over again. I study, I work for guidance, not for belief.

I shall try to explain something schematically, only do not take it literally, but try to understand the principle.

Apart from the Law of Three, already known to you, there is the Law of Seven, which says that nothing remains at rest; each thing moves either in the direction of evolution or in the direction of involution. Only there is a limit to both these movements. In every line of development there are two points where it cannot proceed without extraneous help. In two definite places an additional shock is needed coming from an external force. Everything needs to be pushed at these points; otherwise it cannot continue to move. We find this Law of Seven everywhere—in chemistry, physics, etc.: the same law operates in everything.

The best example of this law is the structure of the musical scale. Let us take a musical octave for explanation. We begin with do. Between it and the next note there is a semitone, and do is able to pass into re. In the same way re is able to pass into mi. But mi does not have this possibility, so something extraneous must give it a shock to make it pass into fa. Fa is able to move on to sol, sol to la, la to si. But just as in the case of mi, si also needs extraneous help.

Every result is a do, not in the course of the process but as an element. Each do is in itself a whole octave. There are a number of musical instruments which can produce seven out of this do. Each of these seven is a do. Every unit has seven units in itself and, upon division, results in another seven units. In dividing do we again obtain do, re, me and so on.

Evolution of food

Man is a three-storied factory. We have said that there are three kinds of food, entering through three different doors.

The first kind of food is what is usually called food: bread, meat, etc.

Each kind of food is a do. In the organism the do passes into other notes. Each do has the possibility of passing into re in the stomach, where the substances of food change their vibrations and their density. These substances are transformed chemically, become mixed, and by means of certain combinations pass into re. Re also has the possibility of passing into mi. But mi cannot evolve by itself. Here the food of the second octave comes to its assistance. The do of the second kind of food, that is, of the second octave, helps mi of the first octave to pass into fa, after which its evolution can proceed further. In its turn, at a similar point, the second octave also requires help from a higher octave. It is helped by a note of the third octave, that is, of the third kind of food—the octave of "impressions."

Thus the first octave evolves up to si. The final substance that the human organism can produce from what is usually called food is si. So the evolution of a piece of bread reaches si. But si cannot develop further in an ordinary man. If si could develop and pass into do of a new octave, it would be possible to build a new body within us. This needs special conditions. Man, by himself, cannot become a new man; special inner combinations are necessary.

Crystallization

When such a special matter accumulates in sufficient quantities, it may begin to crystallize, as salt begins to crystallize in water if more than a certain proportion of it is added. When a great deal of fine matter accumulates in a man, there comes a moment when a new body can form and crystallize in him: the do of a new octave, a higher octave. This body, often called the astral, can only be formed from this special matter and cannot come into being unconsciously. In ordinary conditions, this matter may be produced in the organism, but is used and thrown out.

Ways

To build this body inside man is the aim of all religions and all schools; every religion has its own special way, but the aim is always the same.

There are many ways toward achieving this aim. I have studied about two hundred religions, but if they are to be classified, I would say that there exist only four ways.

Imagine a man as a flat with four rooms. The first room is our physical body and corresponds to the cart in another illustration I have given. The second room is the emotional center, or the horse; the third room, the intellectual center, or the driver; and the fourth room, the master.

Every religion understands that the master is not there and seeks him. But a master can be there only when the whole flat is furnished. Before receiving visitors, all the rooms should be furnished.

Everyone does this in his own way. If a man is not rich, he furnishes every room separately, little by little. In order to furnish the fourth room, one must first furnish the other three. The four ways differ according to the order in which the three rooms are furnished.

The first way begins with the furnishing of the first room, and so on.

The fourth way

The fourth way is the way of "Haida-yoga." It resembles the way of the yogi, but at the same time it has something different.

Like the yogi, the "Haida-yogi" studies everything that can be studied. But he has the means of knowing more than an ordinary yogi can know. In the East there exists a custom: if I know something, I tell it only to my eldest son. In this manner certain secrets are passed on, and outsiders cannot learn them.

Of a hundred yogis perhaps only one knows these secrets. The point is that there is a certain prepared knowledge which speeds up work on the way.

What is the difference? I shall explain with an example. Let us suppose that in order to obtain a certain substance a yogi must do a breathing exercise. He knows that he must lie down and breathe for a certain time. A "Haida-yogi" also knows all that a yogi knows, and does the same as he. But a "Haida-yogi" has a certain apparatus with the help of which he can collect from the air the elements required for his body. A "Haida-yogi" saves time because he knows these secrets.

A yogi spends five hours, a "Haida-yogi" one hour. The latter uses knowledge which the yogi has not got. A yogi does in a year what a "Haida-yogi" does in a month. And so it is in everything.

All these ways aim at one thing—to transform si inwardly into a new body.

Just as a man can build his astral body by an orderly process conforming to law, so he can construct within himself a third body and can then begin to build a fourth body. One body comes into being inside another. They can be separated, and sit on different chairs.

All the ways, all schools have one and the same aim, they always strive for one thing. But a man who has joined one of the ways may not realize this. A monk has faith and thinks that one can only succeed in his way. His teacher alone knows the aim, but he purposely does not tell him, for if his pupil knew he would not work so hard.

Each way has its own theories, its own proofs.

Matter is the same everywhere, but it constantly changes place and enters into different combinations. From the density of a stone to the finest matter, each do has its own emanation, its own atmosphere; for each thing either eats or is eaten. One thing eats another; I eat you, you eat him, and so on.

Everything within man either evolves or involves. An entity is something which remains for a certain duration without involving. Each substance, whether organic or inorganic, can be an entity. Later we shall see that everything is organic. Every entity emanates, sends forth certain matter. This refers equally to the earth, to man, and to the microbe. The earth on which we live has its own emanations, its own atmosphere. Planets are also entities, they also emanate, as do the suns. By means of positive and negative matter new formations resulted from the emanations of the suns. The result of one of these combinations is our earth.

The emanations of every entity have their limits, and therefore each place has a different density of matter. After the act of creation, existence continues, as do emanations. Here on this planet there are emanations of the earth, the planets, and the sun. But the emanations of the earth spread only so far, and beyond that limit there are only emanations coming from the sun and the planets, but not from the earth.

In the region of emanations coming from the earth and the moon, matter is denser; above this region, it is finer. Emanations penetrate everything, according to their possibilities. In this way they reach man.

There are other suns besides ours. Just as I grouped all the planets together, so now I group all the suns and their emanations together. Further than that we can no longer see, but we may logically speak of a world of a higher order. For us it is the last point. It, too, has its own emanations.

According to the Law of Three, matter constantly enters into various combinations, becomes more dense, meets with other matter and becomes still denser, thus changing all its properties and possibilities. For instance, in the higher spheres, intelligence is in its pure form, but as it descends it becomes less intelligent.

Every entity has intelligence, that is, is more or less intelligent. If we take the density of the Absolute as 1, the next density will be 3, or three times more dense, because in God, as in everything, there are three forces. The law is the same everywhere.

The density of the next matter will be twice as great as the density of the second and six times greater than the density of the first matter. The density of the next matter is 12, and in a certain place it is 48. This means that this matter is 48 times heavier, 48 times less intelligent, and so on. We can know the weight of each matter if we know its place. Or, if we know its weight, we shall also know from which place that matter comes.

It is impossible to be impartial, even when nothing touches you on the raw. Such is the law, such is the human psyche. We shall speak later about the why and wherefore of it. In the meantime we shall formulate it thus:

1) the human machine has something that does not allow it to remain impartial, that is, to reason calmly and objectively, without being touched on the raw, and

2) at times it is possible to free oneself from this feature by special efforts.

Concerning this second point I am asking you now to wish to, and to make, this effort, in order that our conversation should not be like all other conversations in ordinary life, that is, mere pouring from the empty into the void, but should be productive both for yourselves and for me.

I called usual conversations pouring from the empty into the void. And indeed, think seriously about the long time each of us has lived in the world and the many conversations we have had! Ask yourselves, look into yourselves—have all those conversations ever led to anything? Do you know anything as surely and indubitably as, for instance, that two and two make four? If you search sincerely in yourselves and give a sincere answer, you will say they have not led to anything.

So our common sense can conclude from past experience that, since this way of talking has so far led to nothing, it will lead to nothing in the future. Even if a man were to live a hundred years, the result would be the same.

Consequently, we must look for the cause of this and if possible change it. Our purpose, then, is to find this cause; so, from the first steps, we shall try to alter our way of carrying on a conversation.

Last time we spoke a little about the Law of Three. I said that this law is everywhere and in everything. It is also found in conversation. For instance, if people talk, one person affirms, another denies. If they don't argue, nothing comes of those affirmations and negations. If they argue, a new result is produced, that is, a new conception unlike that of the man who affirmed or that of the one who denied.

This too is a law, for one cannot altogether say that your former conversations never brought any results. There has been a result, but this result has not been for you but for something or someone outside you.

But now we speak of results in us, or of those we wish to have in us. So, instead of this law acting through us, outside us, we wish to bring it within ourselves, for ourselves. And in order to achieve this we have merely to change the field of action of this law.

What you have done so far when you affirmed, denied and argued with others, I want you now to do with yourselves, so that the results you get may not be objective, as they have been so far, but subjective.

Everything in the world is material and—in accordance with universal law—everything is in motion and is constantly being transformed. The direction of this transformation is from the finest matter to the coarsest, and vice versa.

Between these two limits there are many degrees of density of matter. Moreover, this transformation of matter does not proceed evenly and consecutively.

At some points in the development there are, as it were, stops or transmitting stations. These stations are everything that can be called organisms in the broad sense of the word— the sun, the earth, man and microbe. These stations are commutators which transform matter both in its ascending movement, when it becomes finer, and in its descending movement, toward greater density. This transformation takes place purely mechanically.

Matter is the same everywhere, but at each different level matter has a different density. Therefore each substance has its own place in the general scale of matter, and it is possible to tell whether it is on the way to becoming finer or denser.

Commutators differ only in scale. Man is as much a transmitting station as, for instance, the earth or the sun; he has in him the same mechanical processes. The same transformation goes on in him of higher forms of matter into lower and of lower into higher.

This transformation of substances in two directions, which is called evolution and involution, proceeds not only along the main line from the absolutely fine to the absolutely coarse and vice versa, but at all intermediate stations, on all levels, it branches aside. A substance needed by some entity may be taken by it and absorbed, thus serving the evolution or involution of that entity. Everything absorbs, that is, eats something else, and also itself serves as food. This is what reciprocal exchange means. This reciprocal exchange takes place in everything, in both organic and inorganic matter.

As I have said, everything is in motion. No motion follows a straight line but has simultaneously a twofold direction, circling around itself and falling toward the nearest center of gravity. This is the law of falling which is usually called the law of motion. These universal laws were known in very ancient times. We can come to this conclusion on the basis of historical events which could not have taken place if in the remote past men had not possessed this knowledge. From the most ancient times people knew how to use and control these laws of Nature. This directing of mechanical laws by man is magic and includes not only transformation of substances in the desired direction but also resistance or opposition to certain mechanical influences based on the same laws.

People who know these universal laws and know how to use them are magicians. There is white and black magic. White magic uses its knowledge for good, black magic uses knowledge for evil, for its own selfish purposes.

Like Great Knowledge, magic, which has existed from the most ancient times, has never been lost, and knowledge is always the same. Only the form in which this knowledge was expressed and transmitted changed, depending on the place and the epoch. For instance, now we speak in a language which two hundred years hence will no longer be the same, and two hundred years ago the language was different. In the same way, the form in which the Great Knowledge is expressed is barely comprehensible to subsequent generations and is mostly taken literally. In this way the inner content becomes lost for most people.

In the history of mankind we see two parallel and independent lines of civilization: the esoteric and the exoteric. Invariably one of them overpowers the other and develops while the other fades. A period of esoteric civilization comes when there are favorable external conditions, political and otherwise. Then Knowledge, clothed in the form of a Teaching corresponding to the conditions of time and place, becomes widely spread. Thus it was with Christianity.

But while for some people religion serves as guidance, for others it is only a policeman. Christ, too, was a magician, a man of Knowledge. He was not God, or rather He was God, but on a certain level.

The true meaning and significance of many events in the Gospels are almost forgotten now. For instance, the Last Supper was something quite different from what people usually think. What Christ mixed with bread and wine and gave to the disciples was really his blood.

To explain this I must say something else.

Everything living has an atmosphere around itself. The difference lies only in its size. The larger the organism, the larger its atmosphere. In this respect every organism can be compared to a factory. A factory has an atmosphere around it composed of smoke, steam, waste materials and certain admixtures which evaporate in the process of production. The value of these component parts varies. In exactly the same way, human atmosphere is composed of different elements. And as the atmosphere of different factories has a different smell, so has the atmosphere of different people. For a more sensitive nose, for instance for a dog, it is impossible to confuse the atmosphere of one man with the atmosphere of another.

I have said that man is also a station for transforming substances. Parts of the substances produced in the organism are
used for the transformation of other matters, while other parts
go into his atmosphere, that is, are lost.

So here, too, the same thing happens as in a factory.

Thus the organism works not only for itself, but also for
something else. Men of Knowledge know how to retain the fine
matters in themselves and accumulate them. Only a large accumulation of these fine matters enables a second and lighter
body to be formed within man.

Ordinarily, however, the matters composing man's atmosphere are constantly used up and replaced by man's inner
work.

Man's atmosphere does not necessarily have the shape of a
sphere. It constantly changes its form. In times of strain, of
threat or of danger, it becomes stretched out in the direction
of the strain. Then the opposite side becomes thinner.

Man's atmosphere takes up a certain space. Within the limits of this space it is attracted by the organism, but beyond a
certain limit particles of the atmosphere become torn off and
return no more. This can happen if the atmosphere is greatly
stretched out in one direction.

The same happens when a man moves. Particles of his atmosphere become torn off, are left behind and produce a "trail"
by which a man can be traced. These particles may quickly
mix with the air and dissolve, but they may also stay in place
for a fairly long time. Particles of atmosphere also settle on a
man's clothes, underclothes and other things belonging to him,
so that a kind of track remains between them and the man.

Magnetism, hypnotism and telepathy are phenomena of the
same order. The action of magnetism is direct; the action of
hypnotism is at a short distance through the atmosphere; telepathy is action at a greater distance. Telepathy is analogous to
the telephone or telegraph. In these, the connections are metal
wires, but in telepathy they are the trail of particles left by
man. A man who has the gift of telepathy can fill this trail with

his own matter and thus establish a connection, forming as it were a cable through which he can act on a man's mind. If he possesses some object belonging to a man, then, having thus established a connection, he fashions round this object an image out of wax or clay and, acting upon it, thus acts on the man himself.

Working on oneself is not so difficult as wishing to work, taking the decision. This is so because our centers have to agree among themselves, having realized that, if they are to do anything together, they have to submit to a common master. But it is difficult for them to agree because once there is a master, it will no longer be possible for any of them to order the others about and to do what they like. There is no master in ordinary man. And if there is no master, there is no soul.

A soul—this is the aim of all religions, of all schools. It is only an aim, a possibility; it is not a fact.

Ordinary man has no soul and no will. What is usually called will is merely the resultant of desires. If a man has a desire and at the same time there arises a contrary desire, that is, an unwillingness of greater strength than the first, the second will check the first and extinguish it. This is what in ordinary language is called will.

A child is never born with a soul. A soul can be acquired only in the course of life. Even then it is a great luxury and only for a few. Most people live all their lives without a soul, without a master, and for ordinary life a soul is quite unnecessary.

But a soul cannot be born from nothing. Everything is material and so is the soul, only it consists of very fine matter. Consequently, in order to acquire a soul, it is first of all necessary to have the corresponding matter. Yet we do not have enough materials even for our everyday functions.

Consequently, in order to have the necessary matter or capital, we must begin to economize, so that something may remain over for the next day. For instance, if I am accustomed to eating one potato a day, I may eat only a half and put the other half aside, or I may fast altogether. And the reserve of substances which has to be accumulated must be large; otherwise what there is will soon be dissipated.

If we have some crystals of salt and put them into a glass of water, they will quickly dissolve. More can be added over and over again, and they will still dissolve. But there comes a moment when the solution is saturated. Then the salt no longer dissolves and the crystals remain whole at the bottom.

It is the same with the human organism. Even if materials which are required for the formation of a soul are being constantly produced in the organism, they are dispersed and dissolved in it. There must be a surfeit of such materials in the organism; only then is crystallization possible.

The material crystallized after such a surfeit takes the form of the man's physical body, is a copy of it and may be separated from the physical body. Each body has a different life and each is subject to different orders of laws. The new, or second, body is called the astral body. In relation to the physical body it is what is called the soul. Science is already coming to the possibility of establishing experimentally the existence of the second body.

If we talk about the soul, we must explain that there can be several categories of souls, but that only one of these can truly be called by this word.

A soul, as has been said, is acquired in the course of life. If a man has begun to accumulate these substances, but dies before they have crystallized, then simultaneously with the death of the physical body, these substances also disintegrate and become dispersed.

Man, like every other phenomenon, is the product of three forces.

It must be said that—like everything living—the earth, the planetary world and the sun give out emanations. Out in space between the sun and the earth there are, as it were, three mixtures of emanations. The emanations of the sun, which are longer in proportion to its larger size, reach the earth and even go through it unchecked, since they are the finest. The emanations of the planets reach the earth but do not reach the sun. The emanations of the earth are still shorter. In this way, within the confines of the earth's atmosphere there are three kinds of emanations—those of the sun, of the earth and of the planets. Beyond it there are no emanations of the earth, there are only the emanations of the sun and planets; and higher still there are only the emanations of the sun.

A man is the result of the interaction of planetary emanations and the earth's atmosphere, with matters of the earth. At the death of an ordinary man, his physical body disintegrates into its component parts; the parts from the earth go to the earth. "Dust thou art and unto dust shalt thou return." Parts which came with planetary emanations return to the planetary world; parts from the earth's atmosphere return there. In this way nothing remains as a whole.

If the second body succeeds in becoming crystallized in a man before his death, it can continue to live after the death of the physical body. The matter of this astral body, in its vibrations, corresponds to matter of the sun's emanations and is, theoretically, indestructible within the confines of the earth and its atmosphere. All the same, the duration of its life can be different. It can live a long time or its existence can end very quickly. This is because, like the first, the second body also has centers; it also lives and also receives impressions. And since it lacks sufficient experience and material of impressions it must, like a newborn baby, receive a certain education. Otherwise it is helpless and cannot exist independently, and very soon disintegrates like the physical body.

Everything that exists is subject to the same law, for "as above, so below." What can exist in one set of conditions cannot exist in another. If the astral body comes up against matter of finer vibrations it disintegrates.

And so, to the question "Is the soul immortal?," in general it is only possible to answer "yes and no." To answer more definitely, we must know what kind of soul is meant and what kind of immortality.

As I have said, the second body of man is the soul in relation to the physical body. Although in itself it is also divided into three principles, taken as a whole it represents the active force, the positive principle in relation to the passive, negative principle which is the physical body. The neutralizing principle between them is a special magnetism, which is not possessed by everyone but without which it is impossible for the second body to be master of the first.

Further development is possible. A man with two bodies can acquire new properties by the crystallization of new substances. A third body is then formed within the second, which is sometimes called the mental body. The third body will then be the active principle; the second, the neutralizing; and the first, the physical body, the passive principle.

But this is still not soul in the real meaning of the word. At the death of the physical body, the astral may also die and the mental body may remain alone. But, although in a certain sense it is immortal, it too can die sooner or later.

Only the fourth body completes all the development possible for man in the earthly conditions of his existence. It is immortal within the limits of the solar system. Real will belongs to this body. It is the real "I," the soul of man, the master. It is the active principle in relation to the other bodies taken together.

All four bodies, which fit one into another, may be separated. After the death of the physical body, the higher bodies may become divided.

Reincarnation is a very rare phenomenon. It is possible either over a very long period of time, or in the event of there being a man whose physical body is identical with that of the man who possessed these higher bodies. Moreover, the astral body can reincarnate only if it accidentally meets with such a physical body, but this can happen only unconsciously. But the mental body is able to choose.

V

*Music played during exercises diverts the movement innate
in us which in life is the chief source of interference. Music
alone cannot separate the whole of our unconscious automatism, but it is one of the aids to this. Music cannot draw
away the whole of our mechanicalness, but for the moment,
owing to the absence of other means, we shall use only
music.*

*One thing is important: while performing all the given
external tasks to the accompaniment of music, you must
learn from the beginning not to pay attention to the music
but to listen to it automatically. At first, attention will stray
to the music from time to time, but later it will be possible
to listen to music and other things entirely with automatic
attention, the nature of which is different.*

*It is important to learn to distinguish this attention from
mechanical attention. As long as the two attentions are not
separated from one another they remain so alike that an
ignorant person is unable to distinguish between them. Full,
deep, highly concentrated attention makes it possible
to separate the one from the other. Learn to know the
difference between these two kinds of attention by taste
in order to discriminate between our incoming thoughts,
information on one side and differentiation on the other.*

(Prieuré, January 20, 1923)

To all my questions, "Has anyone thought, while working today, about yesterday's lecture?" I invariably receive the same answer—they forgot. And yet to think while working is the same as to remember oneself.

It is impossible to remember oneself. And people do not remember because they wish to live by mind alone. Yet the store of attention in the mind (like the electric charge of a battery) is very small. And other parts of the body have no wish to remember.

Maybe you remember it being said that man is like a rig consisting of passenger, driver, horse and carriage. Except there can be no question of the passenger, for he is not there, so we can only speak of the driver. Our mind is the driver.

This mind of ours wants to do something, has set itself the task of working differently from the way it worked before, of remembering itself. All the interests we have related to self-change, self-alteration, belong only to the driver, that is, are only mental.

As regards feeling and body—these parts are not in the least interested in putting self-remembering into practice. And yet the main thing is to change not in the mind, but in the parts that are not interested. The mind can change quite easily. Attainment is not reached through the mind; if it is reached through the mind it is of no use at all.

Therefore one should teach, and learn, not through the mind but through the feelings and the body. At the same time feeling and body have no language; they have neither the language nor the understanding we possess. They understand neither Russian nor English; the horse does not understand the language of the driver, nor the carriage that of the horse. If the driver says in English, "Turn right," nothing will happen. The horse understands the language of the reins and will turn right only obeying the reins. Or another horse will turn without reins if you rub it in an accustomed place—as for instance, donkeys in Persia are trained. The same with the carriage—it has its own structure. If the shafts turn right, the rear wheels go left. Then another movement and the wheels go right. This is because the carriage only understands this movement and reacts to it in its own way. So the driver should know the weak sides, or the characteristics, of the carriage. Only then can he drive it in the direction he wishes. But if he merely sits on his box and says in his own language "go right" or "go left," the team will not budge even if he shouts for a year.

We are an exact replica of such a team. Mind alone cannot be called a man, just as a driver who sits in a pub cannot be called a driver who fulfills his function. Our mind is like a professional cabby who sits at home or in a pub and drives passengers to different places, in his dreams. Just as his driving is not real, so trying to work with the mind alone will lead nowhere. One will only become a professional, a lunatic.

The power of changing oneself lies not in the mind, but in the body and the feelings. Unfortunately, however, our body and our feelings are so constituted that they don't care a jot about anything so long as they are happy. They live for the moment and their memory is short. The mind alone lives for tomorrow. Each has its own merits. The merit of the mind is that it looks ahead. But it is only the other two that can "do."

Until now, until today, the greater part of desire and striving was accidental, only in the mind. This means that the de-

sire exists in the mind alone. So far, in the minds of those present there arose accidentally a desire to attain something, to
change something. But only in the mind. But nothing has
changed in them yet. There is only this bare idea in the head,
but each has remained as he was. Even if he works ten years
with his mind, if he studies day and night, remembers in his
mind and strives, he will achieve nothing useful or real, because in the mind there is nothing to change; what must
change is the horse's disposition. Desire must be in the horse,
and ability in the carriage.

But, as we have said already, the difficulty is that, owing to
wrong modern upbringing and the fact that the lack of
connection in us between body, feeling and mind has not been
recognized from childhood, the majority of people are so deformed that there is no common language between one part
and another. This is why it is so difficult for us to establish a
connection between them, and still more difficult to force our
parts to change their way of living. This is why we are obliged
to make them communicate, but not in the language given us
by nature, which would have been easy and by means of
which our parts would very soon have become reconciled to
one another, would have come to an accord and, by concerted
efforts and understanding, would have attained the desired
aim common to them all.

In most of us this common language I speak about is irre-
trievably lost. The only thing left us is to establish a connection in a roundabout, "fraudulent" way. And these indirect,
"fraudulent," artificial connections must be very subjective,
since they must depend on a man's character and the form his
inner makeup has taken.

So now we must establish this subjectivity, and find a program of work, in order to make connections with the other
parts. Establishing this subjectivity is also complicated; it cannot be arrived at at once, not until a man is thoroughly ana-
lyzed and pulled to pieces, not until one has probed "as far as
his grandmother."

Therefore on the one hand we shall go on establishing this

subjectivity for each man separately, and on the other we shall begin general work possible for everyone—practical exercises. There are certain subjective methods and there are general methods. So we shall try to find subjective methods and at the same time try to apply general methods.

Bear in mind that subjective directions will be given only to those who will prove themselves, who will show that they can work and don't idle. General methods, general occupations will be accessible to all, but subjective methods will be given in groups only to those who work, who try and wish to try to work with their whole being. Those who are lazy, who trust to luck, will never see or hear that which constitutes real work, even if they remain here for ten years.

Those who heard lectures must have already heard of, thought about and tried the so-called "self-remembering." Those who have tried have probably found that, in spite of great efforts and desire, this self-remembering, so understandable to the mind, intellectually so easily possible and admissible, is, in actual practice, impossible. And indeed it is impossible.

When we say "remember yourself," we mean yourself. But we ourselves, my "I," are—my feelings, my body, my sensations. I myself am not my mind, not my thought. Our mind is not us—it is merely a small part of us. It is true that this part has a connection with us, but only a small connection, and so very little material is allotted to it by our organization. If our body and feelings receive for their existence the necessary energy and various elements in the proportion of say, twenty parts, our mind receives only one part. Our attention is the product evolved from these elements, this material. Our separate parts have different attention; its duration and its power are proportionate to the material received. The part which receives more material has more attention.

Since our mind is fed by less material, its attention, that is, its memory, is short and it is effective only as long as the material for it lasts. Indeed, if we wish (and continue to wish) to remember ourselves only with our mind, we shall be unable to remember ourselves longer than our material allows, no matter how much we may dream about it, no matter how much we may wish it or what measures we take. When this material is spent, our attention vanishes.

It is exactly like an accumulator for lighting purposes. It will make a lamp burn as long as it is charged. When the energy is spent the lamp cannot give any light even if it is in order and the wiring in good repair. The light of the lamp is our memory. This should explain why a man cannot remember himself longer. And indeed he cannot because this particular memory is short and will always be short. It is so arranged.

It is impossible to install a bigger accumulator or to fill it with a greater amount of energy than it can hold. But it is possible to increase our self-remembering, not by enlarging our accumulator but by bringing in other parts with their own accumulators and making them participate in the general work. If this is achieved, all our parts will lend a hand and mutually help one another in keeping the desired general light burning.

Since we have confidence in our mind and our mind has come to the conclusion that it is good and necessary for our other parts, we must do all we can to arouse their interest and try to convince them that the desired achievement is useful and necessary for them too.

I must admit that the greater part of our total "I" is not in the least interested in self-remembering. More than that, it does not even suspect the existence of this desire in its brother—thought. Consequently we must try to acquaint them with these desires. If they conceive a desire to work in this direction, half the work is done; we can begin teaching and helping them.

Unfortunately one cannot speak to them intelligently at once because, owing to careless upbringing, the horse and the carriage don't know any language fitting for a well-brought-up man. Their life and their thinking are instinctive, as in an animal, and so it is impossible to prove to them logically where their future profit lies or explain all their possibilities. For the present it is only possible to make them start working by round-about, "fraudulent" methods. If this is done they may possibly develop common sense. Logic and common sense are not foreign to them, but they received no education. They are like a man who has been made to live away from his fellowmen, without any communication with them. Such a man cannot think logically as we do. We have this capacity because from childhood we have lived among other men and have had to deal with them. Like this man, isolated from others, our parts lived by animal instincts, without thought and logic. Owing to this, these capacities have degenerated, the qualities given them by nature have become dulled and atrophied. But in view of their original nature, this atrophy has no irreparable consequences and it is possible to bring them back to life in their original form.

Naturally, a great deal of labor is needed to destroy the crust of vices—consequences—already formed. So, instead of starting new work, it is necessary to correct old sins.

For example, I wish to remember myself as long as possible. But I have proved to myself that I very quickly forget the task I set myself, because my mind has very few associations connected with it.

I have noticed that other associations engulf the associations connected with self-remembering. Our associations take place in our formatory apparatus owing to shocks which the formatory apparatus receives from the centers. Each shock has associations of its own particular character; their strength depends on the material which produces them.

If the thinking center produces associations of self-remembering, incoming associations of another character, which come from other parts and have nothing to do with self-remembering, absorb these desirable associations, since they come from many different places and so are more numerous.

And so here I sit.

My problem is to bring my other parts to a point where my thinking center would be able to prolong the state of self-remembering as much as possible, without exhausting the energy immediately.

It should be pointed out here that self-remembering, however full and whole, can be of two kinds, conscious and mechanical—remembering oneself consciously and remembering oneself by associations. Mechanical, that is, associative self-remembering can bring no essential profit, yet such associative self-remembering is of tremendous value in the beginning. Later it should not be used, for such a self-remembering, however complete, does not result in any real, concrete doing. But in the beginning it too is necessary.

There exists another, a conscious, self-remembering which is not mechanical.

Now I am sitting here. I am totally unable to remember myself and I have no idea of it. But I have heard about it. A friend of mine proved to me today that it is possible.

Then I thought about it and became convinced that if I could remember myself long enough I would make fewer mistakes and would do more things that are desirable.

Now I wish to remember, but every rustle, every person, every sound distracts my attention, and I forget.

Before me is a sheet of paper on which I deliberately wrote it, in order that this paper should act for me as a shock for remembering myself. But the paper has proved of no help. So long as my attention is concentrated on this paper I remember. As soon as my attention becomes distracted I look at the paper, but I cannot remember myself.

I try another way. I repeat to myself, "I wish to remember myself." But this does not help either. At moments I notice that I repeat it mechanically, but my attention is not there.

I try in every possible way. For instance, I sit and try to associate certain physical discomforts with self-remembering. For example, my corn aches. But the corn helps only for a short time; later this corn begins to be felt purely mechanically.

[228]

Still I try all possible means, for I have a great desire to succeed in remembering myself.

In order to know how to proceed, I would be interested to know who has thought as I have and who has tried in a similar way?

Supposing I have not yet tried in this way. Supposing till now I have always tried directly by the mind. I have not yet tried to create in myself associations of another nature as well, associations which are not only those of the thinking center. I wish to try; maybe the result will be better. Maybe I shall understand more quickly about the possibility of something different.

I wish to remember—at this moment I remember.

I remember by my mind. I ask myself: do I remember by sensation as well? As a matter of fact I find that by sensation I do not remember myself.

What is the difference between sensation and feeling?

Does everyone understand?

For example, here I sit. Owing to my unaccustomed posture my muscles are unusually tensed. As a rule I have no sensation of my muscles in my established customary posture. Like everyone else I have a limited number of postures. But now I have taken a new, unusual position. I have a sensation of my body, if not the whole of it, at least of some parts of my body, of warmth, of the circulation of the blood. As I sit I feel that behind me there is a hot stove. Since it is warm behind and cold in front, there is a great difference in the air, so I never cease to sense myself thanks to this external contrasting difference of the air.

Tonight I had rabbit for supper. Since the rabbit and the *ha-bur-chubur* were very good I ate too much. I sense my stomach and my breathing is unusually heavy. I sense the whole time.

Just now I have been preparing a dish with A. and have put it in the oven. While I was preparing it, I remembered how my mother used to prepare this dish. I remembered my mother and remembered certain moments connected with this. These memories aroused feeling in me. I feel these moments and my feeling does not leave me.

Now I look at this lamp. When there was as yet no lighting in the Study House I thought that I needed precisely this kind of light. At that time I made a plan of what was required to obtain this kind of lighting. It was done, and this is the result. When the light was switched on and I saw it, I had a feeling of self-satisfaction; and the feeling, which was aroused then, continues—I feel this self-satisfaction.

A moment ago I was walking from the Turkish bath. It was dark and, as I could not see in front of me, I hit a tree. I remembered by association how, on one occasion, I was walking in similar darkness and collided with a man. I received the impact of this collision in my chest, so I let fly and hit the unknown man who had run into me. Later I found out that the man was not to blame; yet I hit him so hard that he lost several teeth. At the moment I had not thought that the man who had run into me might be innocent, but when I had calmed down, I understood. When later I saw this innocent man in the street, with his disfigured face, I was so sorry for him that when I remember him now I experience the same pang of conscience I felt then. And now, when I hit the tree, this feeling came to life in me again. I again saw before me the unhappy, bruised face of this good man.

I have given you examples of six different inner states. Three of them relate to the moving center and three to the emotional center. In ordinary language all six are called feelings. Yet in right classification those whose nature is connected with the moving center should be called sensations, and those whose nature is connected with emotional center, feelings. There are thousands of different sensations which are usually called feelings. They are all different, their material is different, their effects different and their causes different.

In examining them more closely we can establish their nature and give them corresponding names. They are often so different in their nature that they have nothing whatever in common. Some originate in one place, others in another place. In some people one place of origin (of a given kind of sensations) is absent, in others another place of origin may be lacking. In yet other people, all may be present.

The time will come when we shall endeavor to shut off artificially one, or two, or several together, to learn their real nature.

At present we must have an idea of two different experiences, one of which we shall agree to call "feeling" and the other "sensation." We shall call "feeling" the one whose place of origin is what we call the emotional center; while "sensations" are those so-called feelings whose place of origin is in what we call the moving center. Now, of course, each one must understand and examine his sensations and feelings and learn approximately the difference between them.

For primary exercises in self-remembering the participation of all three centers is necessary, and we began to speak of the difference between feelings and sensations because it is necessary to have simultaneously both feeling and sensation.

We can come to this exercise only with the participation of thought. The first thing is thought. We already know this. We desire, we wish; therefore our thoughts can be more or less easily adapted to this work, because we have already had practical experience of them.

At the beginning all three need to be evoked artificially. In the case of our thoughts the means of artificially evoking them is conversations, lectures and so on. For example, if nothing is said, nothing is evoked. Readings, talks have served as an artificial shock. I call it artificial because I was not born with these desires, they are not natural, they are not an organic necessity. These desires are artificial and their consequences will be equally artificial.

And if thoughts are artificial, then I can create in myself for this purpose sensations which are also artificial.

I repeat: artificial things are necessary only in the beginning. The fullness of what we desire cannot be attained artificially, but, for beginning, this way is necessary.

I take the easiest, most simple thing: I wish to start trying with what is simplest. In my thoughts I already have a certain number of associations for self-remembering, especially thanks to the fact that here we have suitable conditions and a suitable place, and are surrounded with people who have the same aims. Owing to all this, in addition to the associations I already have, I shall continue to form new ones. Consequently I am more or less assured that on this side I shall have reminders and shocks, and therefore I shall pay little attention to thoughts, but shall chiefly concern myself with the other parts and shall devote all my time to them.

The simplest, most accessible sensation, for the beginning, can be got through uncomfortable postures. Now I am sitting as I never sat before. For a time it is all right, but after a while I develop an ache; a strange, unaccustomed sensation starts in my legs. In the first place I am convinced that the ache is not harmful and will lead to no harmful consequences, but is merely an unaccustomed and therefore unpleasant sensation.

In order better to understand the sensations I am going to speak about, I think it would be best if from this moment you all assumed some uncomfortable position.

I have all the time an urge to shift about, to move my legs in order to change the uncomfortable position. But I have for the present undertaken the task to bear it, to keep a "stop" of the whole body, except my head.

For the moment I wish to forget about self-remembering. Now I wish temporarily to concentrate all my attention, all my thoughts, on not allowing myself automatically, unconsciously, to change my position.

Let us direct our attention to the following: at first the legs begin to ache, then this sensation begins to rise higher and higher, so the region of pain widens. Let the attention pass on to the back. Is there a place where a special sensation is localized? Only he can sense this who has indeed assumed an uncomfortable, unaccustomed position.

Now, when an unpleasant sensation in the body, especially in certain places, has already resulted, I begin to think in my mind: "I wish. I wish very much to be able often to recollect, in order to remember that it is necessary to remember myself. I wish! You—it is me, it is my body." I say to my body: "You. You—me. You are also me. I wish!"

These sensations which my body is now experiencing—and every similar sensation—I wish them to remind me. "I wish! You are me. I wish! I wish to recollect as often as possible that I wish to remember, that I wish to remember myself."

My legs have gone to sleep. I get up.

"I wish to remember."

Let those who also wish get up. "I wish to remember often."

All these sensations will remind me.

Now our sensations will begin to change in different degrees. Let each degree, each change in these sensations remind me of self-remembering. Think, walk. Walk about, and think. My uncomfortable state has now gone.

I assume another position.

First: *I* 2nd: *wish* 3rd: *to remember* 4th: *myself.*

I—simply "I" mentally.

Wish—I feel. Remember now the vibrations which occur in your body when you set yourself a task for the next day. A sensation similar to the one which will occur tomorrow when you are performing your task should take place in you now in a lesser degree. I wish to remember the sensation. For instance, I wish to go and lie down. I experience a pleasant sensation together with my thought about it. At this moment I experience this pleasant sensation in my whole body, in a lesser degree. If one pays attention, it is possible clearly to see this vibration in oneself. For this, one has to pay attention to what kinds of sensations arise in the body. At the present moment we need to understand the taste of the sensation of mental wishing.

When you pronounce these four words—"I wish to remember myself"—I wish you to experience what I am now going to speak about.

When you pronounce the word "*I*" you will have a purely subjective sensation in the head, the chest, the back, according to the state you are in at the moment. I must not say "I" merely mechanically, as a word, but I must note in myself its resonance. This means that in saying "I" you must listen carefully to the inner sensation and watch so as never once to say the word "I" automatically, no matter how often you say it.

The second word is "*wish*." Sense with your whole body the vibration which occurs in you.

"*To remember*." Every man, when he remembers, has a barely perceptible process in the middle of the chest.

"*Myself*." When I say "myself," I mean the whole of myself. Usually, when I say the word "myself," I am accustomed to mean either thought, or feeling or body. Now we must take the whole, the atmosphere, the body and all that is in it.

All the four words, each one by itself, has its own nature and its own place of resonance.

If all the four words were to resound in one and the same place, it would never be possible for all four to resound with equal intensity. Our centers are like galvanic batteries from which current flows for a certain time if a button is pressed. Then it stops and the button has to be released to enable the galvanic battery to refill itself with electricity.

But in our centers the expenditure of energy is still quicker than in a galvanic battery. These centers of ours, which produce a resonance when we pronounce each of the four words, must be given rest in turn, if they are to be able to respond. Each of the bells possesses its own battery. While I am saying "I," one bell answers; "wish," another bell; "to remember," a third bell; "myself," the general bell.

Some time ago it was said that each center has its own accumulator. At the same time our machine has a general accumulator, independent of the accumulators belonging to the centers. The energy in this general accumulator is generated only when all accumulators work one after another in a certain definite combination. By this means the general accumulator is charged. In this case, the general accumulator becomes an accumulator in the full sense of the word, for reserve energy is collected and stored there during the moments when a certain energy is not being spent.

A feature common to us all is that the accumulators of our centers are refilled with energy only insofar as it is being spent, so that no energy remains in them beyond the amount being expended.

To prolong the memory of self-remembering is possible by making the energy stored in us last longer, if we are able to manufacture a store of this energy.

The two rivers

It will be useful if we compare human life in general to a large river which arises from various sources and flows into two separate streams, that is to say, there occurs in this river a dividing of the waters, and we can compare the life of any one man to one of the drops of water composing this river of life.

On account of the unbecoming life of people, it was established for the purposes of the common actualizing of everything existing that, in general, human life on the Earth should flow in two streams. Great Nature foresaw and gradually fixed in the common presence of humanity a corresponding property, so that, before the dividing of the waters, in each drop that has this corresponding inner subjective "struggle with one's own denying part," there might arise that "something," thanks to which certain properties are acquired which give the possibility, at the place of the branching of the waters of life, of entering one or the other stream.

Thus there are two directions in the life of humanity: active and passive. Laws are the same everywhere. These two laws, these two currents, continually meet, now crossing each other, now running parallel. But they never mix; they support each other, they are indispensable for each other.

It was always so and so it will remain.

Now, the life of all ordinary men taken together can be

[236]

thought of as one of these rivers in which each life, whether of a man or of any other living being, is represented by a drop in the river, and the river in itself is a link in the cosmic chain.

In accordance with general cosmic laws, the river flows in a fixed direction. All its turns, all its bends, all these changes have a definite purpose. In this purpose every drop plays a part insofar as it is part of the river, but the law of the river as a whole does not extend to the individual drops. The changes of position, movement and direction of the drops are completely accidental. At one moment a drop is here; the next moment it is there; now it is on the surface, now it has gone to the bottom. Accidentally it rises, accidentally it collides with another and descends; now it moves quickly, now slowly. Whether its life is easy or difficult depends on where it happens to be. There is no individual law for it, no personal fate. Only the whole river has a fate, which is common to all the drops. Personal sorrow and joy, happiness and suffering—in that current, all these are accidental.

But the drop has, in principle, a possibility of escaping from this general current and jumping across to the other, the neighboring, stream.

This too is a law of Nature. But, for this, the drop must know how to make use of accidental shocks, and of the momentum of the whole river, so as to come to the surface and be closer to the bank at those places where it is easier to jump across. It must choose not only the right place but also the right time, to make use of winds, currents and storms. Then the drop has a chance to rise with the spray and jump across into the other river.

From the moment it gets into the other river, the drop is in a different world, in a different life, and therefore is under different laws. In this second river a law exists for individual drops, the law of alternating progression. A drop comes to the top or goes to the bottom, this time not by accident but by law. On coming to the surface, the drop gradually becomes heavier and sinks; deep down it loses weight and rises again.

To float on the surface is good for it—to be deep down is bad. Much depends here on skill and on effort. In this second river there are different currents and it is necessary to get into the required current. The drop must float on the surface as long as possible in order to prepare itself, to earn the possibility of passing into another current, and so on.

But we are in the first river. As long as we are in this passive current it will carry us wherever it may; as long as we are passive we shall be pushed about and be at the mercy of every accident. We are the slaves of these accidents.

At the same time Nature has given us the possibility of escaping from this slavery. Therefore when we talk about freedom we are talking precisely about crossing over into the other river.

But of course it is not so simple—you cannot cross over merely because you wish. Strong desire and long preparation are necessary. You will have to live through being identified with all the attractions in the first river. You must die to this river. All religions speak about this death: "Unless you die, you cannot be born again."

This does not mean physical death. From that death there is no necessity to rise again because if there is a soul, and it is immortal, it can get along without the body, the loss of which we call death. And the reason for rising again is not in order to appear before the Lord God on the day of judgment as the fathers of the Church teach us. No, Christ and all the others spoke of the death which can take place in life, the death of the tyrant from whom our slavery comes, that death which is a necessary condition of the first and principal liberation of man.

If a man were deprived of his illusions and all that prevents him from seeing reality—if he were deprived of his interests, his cares, his expectations and hopes—all his strivings would collapse, everything would become empty and there would remain an empty being, an empty body, only physiologically alive.

This would be the death of "I," the death of everything it consisted of, the destruction of everything false collected through ignorance or inexperience. All this will remain in him merely as material, but subject to selection. Then a man will be able to choose for himself and not have imposed on him what others like. He will have conscious choice.

This is difficult. No, difficult is not the word. The word "impossible" is also wrong, because, in principle, it is possible; only it is a thousand times more difficult than to become a multimillionaire through honest work.

Question: There are two rivers—how can a drop go from the first to the second?

Answer: It must buy a ticket. It is necessary to realize that only he can cross who has some real possibility of changing. This possibility depends on desire, strong wish of a very special kind, wishing with the essence, not with the personality. You must understand that it is very difficult to be sincere with yourself, and a man is very much afraid of seeing the truth.

Sincerity is a function of conscience. Every man has a conscience—it is a property of normal human beings. But owing to civilization this function has become crusted over and has ceased to work, except in special circumstances where the associations are very strong. Then, it functions for a little time and disappears again. Such moments are due to strong shock, great sorrow, or insult. At these times conscience unites personality and essence, which otherwise are altogether separate.

This question about two rivers refers to essence, as all real things do. Your essence is permanent; your personality is your education, your ideas, your beliefs—things caused by your environment; these you acquire, and can lose. The object of these talks is to help you to get something real. But now we cannot ask this question seriously; we must first ask: "How can I prepare myself to ask this question?"

I suppose that some understanding of your personality has led you to a certain dissatisfaction with your life as it is, and to the hope of finding something better. You hope that I will tell you something you do not know which will show you the first step.

Try to understand that what you usually call "I" is not I; there are many "I's" and each "I" has a different wish. Try to verify this. You wish to change, but which part of you has this wish? Many parts of you want many things, but only one part is real. It will be very useful for you to try to be sincere with yourself. Sincerity is the key which will open the door through which you will see your separate parts, and you will see something quite new. You must go on trying to be sincere. Each day you put on a mask, and you must take it off little by little.

But there is one important thing to realize. Man cannot free himself; he cannot observe himself all the time; perhaps he can for five minutes, but really to know himself he must know how he spends his whole day. Also, man has only one attention; he cannot always see new things, but he can sometimes make discoveries by accident, and these he can recognize again. There is this peculiarity: when you once discover a thing in yourself—you see it again. But, because man is mechanical, he can very rarely see his weakness. When you see something new, you get an image of it, and afterwards you see this thing with the same impression, which may be right or wrong. If you hear of someone before you see him, you make up an image of him, and if it bears any resemblance to the original, this image and not the reality is photographed. We very rarely see what we look at.

Man is a personality full of prejudices. There are two kinds of prejudice: prejudice of essence and prejudice of personality. Man knows nothing, he lives under authority, he accepts and believes all influences. We know nothing. We fail to differentiate when a man is speaking on a subject he really knows, and when he is talking nonsense—we believe it all. We have nothing of our own; everything that we put in our pocket is not our own—and on the inside, we have nothing.

And in our essence we have almost nothing, because from the time we were babies we have absorbed almost nothing.

Except that, by accident, sometimes something may enter.

We have in our personality perhaps twenty or thirty ideas we have picked up. We forget where we got them, but when something like one of these ideas comes along, we think we understand it. It is just an imprint on the brain. We are really slaves, and we set one prejudice against another.

Essence has a similar impressionability. For example we spoke about colors, and said that everybody has a special color he cherishes. These partialities are also acquired mechanically.

Now, as to the question. I can put it this way. Suppose you find a teacher with real knowledge who wishes to help you, and you wish to learn: even so, he cannot help you. He can only do so when you wish in the right way. This must be your aim; but this aim is also too far off, it is necessary to find what will bring you to it or at least bring you nearer to it. The aim must be divided. So, we must have as our aim the capacity to wish, and this can only be attained by a man who realizes his nothingness. We must revalue our values, and this must be based on need. Man cannot do this revaluation by himself alone.

I can advise you, but I cannot help you; nor can the Institute help you. It can only help you when you are on the Way —but you are not there.

First you must decide: is the Way necessary for you or not? How are you to begin to find this out? If you are serious, you must change your point of view, you must think in a new way, you must find your possible aim. This you cannot do alone, you must call on a friend who can help you—everyone can help—but especially two friends can help each other to revalue their values.

It is very difficult to be sincere all at once, but, if you try, you will improve gradually. When you can be sincere, I can show you, or help you to see, the things you are afraid of, and you will find what is necessary and useful for yourself. These values really can change. Your mind can change every day, but your essence stays as it is.

But there is a risk. Even this preparation of the mind gives results. Occasionally a man may feel with his essence something which is very bad for him, or at least for his peace of mind. He has already tasted something and, though he forgets, it may return. If it is very strong, your associations will keep reminding you of it and, if it is intense, you will be half in one place and half in another, and you will never be quite comfortable. This is good only if a man has a real possibility of change, and the chance of changing. People can be very unhappy, neither fish nor flesh nor herring. It is a serious risk. Before you think of changing your seat you would be wise to consider very carefully and take a good look at both kinds of chairs. Happy is the man who sits in his ordinary chair. A thousand times happier is the man who sits in the chair of the angels, but miserable is the man who has no chair. You must decide—is it worthwhile? Examine the chairs, revalue your values.

The first aim is to forget all about everything else, talk to your friend, study and examine the chairs. But I warn you, when you start looking you will find much that is bad in your present chair.

Next time, if you have made up your mind what you are going to decide about your life, I can talk differently on this subject. Try to see yourself, for you do not know yourself. You must realize this risk; the man who tries to see himself can be very unhappy, for he will see much that is bad, much that he will wish to change—and that change is very difficult. It is easy to start, but, once you have given up your chair, it is very difficult to get another, and it may cause great unhappiness. Everyone knows the gnawings of remorse. Now your conscience is relative, but when you change your values you will have to stop lying to yourself. When you have seen one thing, it is much easier to see another, and it is more difficult to shut your eyes. You must either stop looking or be willing to take risks.

There are two kinds of love: one, the love of a slave; the other, which must be acquired by work. The first has no value at all; only the second has value, that is, love acquired through work. This is the love about which all religions speak.

If you love when "it" loves, it does not depend on you and so has no merit. It is what we call the love of a slave. You love even when you should not love. Circumstances make you love mechanically.

Real love is Christian, religious love; with that love no one is born. For this love you must work. Some know it from childhood, others only in old age. If somebody has real love, he acquired it during his life. But it is very difficult to learn. And it is impossible to begin learning directly, on people. Every man touches another on the raw, makes you put on brakes and gives you very little chance to try.

Love may be of different kinds. To understand what kind of love we are speaking about, it is necessary to define it.

Now we are speaking about love for life. Wherever there is life—beginning with plants (for they too have life), animals, in a word wherever life exists, there is love. Each life is a representative of God. Whoever can see the representative will see Him who is represented. Every life is sensitive to love. Even inanimate things such as flowers, which have no consciousness, understand whether you love them or not. Even unconscious life reacts in a corresponding way to each man, and responds to him according to his reactions.

As you sow, so you reap, and not only in the sense that if you sow wheat you will get wheat. The question is how you sow. It can literally turn to straw. On the same ground, different people can sow the same seeds and the results will be different. But these are only seeds. Man is certainly more sensitive to what is sown in him than a seed. Animals are also very sensitive, although less so than man. For instance, X. was sent to look after the animals. Many became ill and died, the hens laid fewer eggs, and so on. Even a cow will give less milk if you do not love her. The difference is quite startling.

Man is more sensitive than a cow, but unconsciously. And so if you feel antipathy or hate another person, it is only because somebody has sown something bad in you. Whoever wishes to learn to love his neighbor must begin by trying to love plants and animals. Whoever does not love life does not love God. To begin straightaway by trying to love a man is impossible, because the other man is like you, and he will hit back at you. But an animal is mute and will sadly resign itself. That is why it is easier to start practicing on animals.

It is very important for a man who works on himself to understand that change can take place in him only if he changes his attitude to the outside world. In general you don't know what must be loved and what must not be loved, because all that is relative. With you, one and the same thing is loved and not loved; but there are objective things which we must love or must not love. Therefore it is more productive and practical to forget about what you call good and bad and begin to act only when you have learned to choose for yourself.

Now if you want to work on yourself, you must work out in yourself different kinds of attitudes. Except with big and more clear-cut things which are undeniably bad, you have to exercise yourselves in this way: if you like a rose, try to dislike it; if you dislike it, try to like it. It is best to begin with the world of plants; try from tomorrow to look at plants in a way you have not looked before. Every man is attracted toward certain plants, and not by others. Perhaps we have not noticed that till now. First you have to look, then put another in its place and then notice and try to understand why this attraction or aversion is there. I am sure that everyone feels something or senses something. It is a process which takes place in the subconscious, and the mind does not see it, but if you begin to look consciously, you will see many things, you will discover many Americas. Plants, like man, have relations between themselves, and relations exist also between plants and men, but they change from time to time. All living things are tied one to another. This includes everything that lives. All things depend on each other.

Plants act on a man's moods and the mood of a man acts on the mood of a plant. As long as we live we shall make experiments. Even living flowers in a pot will live or die according to the mood.

Question: Has free will a place in your teaching?

Answer: Free will is the function of the real I, of him whom we call the Master. He who has a Master has will. He who has not has no will. What is ordinarily called will is an adjustment between willingness and unwillingness. For instance, the mind wants something and the feeling does not want it; if the mind proves to be stronger than the feeling, a man obeys his mind. In the opposite case, he will obey his feelings. This is what is called "free will" in an ordinary man. An ordinary man is ruled now by the mind, now by the feeling, now by the body. Very often he obeys orders coming from the automatic apparatus; a thousand times more often he is ordered about by the sex center.

Real free will can only be when one I always directs, when man has a Master for his team. An ordinary man has no master; the carriage constantly changes passengers and each passenger calls himself I.

Nevertheless, free will is a reality, it does exist. But we, as we are, cannot have it. A real man can have it.

Question: Are there no people who have free will?

[246]

Answer: I am speaking of the majority of men. Those who have will—have will. Anyway, free will is not an ordinary phenomenon. It cannot be had for the asking, cannot be bought in a shop.

Question: What is the attitude of your teaching to morality?

Answer: Morality can be subjective or objective. Objective morality is the same throughout the earth; subjective morality is different everywhere and everybody defines it differently: what is good for one is bad for another, and vice versa. Morality is a stick with two ends—it can be turned this way and that way.

From the time when man began to live on the earth, from the time of Adam—with the help of God, Nature, and all our surroundings—there gradually formed in us an organ, the function of which is conscience. Every man has this organ, and whoever is guided by conscience automatically behaves in accordance with the Commandments. If our conscience were open and pure, there would be no need to speak about morality. Then, unconsciously or consciously, everyone would behave according to the dictates of this inner voice.

Conscience is not a stick with two ends. It is the quite definite realization, formed in us through the ages, of what is good and what is bad. Unfortunately, for many reasons, this organ is usually covered over with a kind of crust.

Question: What can break the crust?

Answer: Only intense suffering or shock pierces the crust, and then conscience speaks; but after a while a man calms down and the organ becomes covered over once more. A strong shock is needed for the organ to become uncovered automatically.

For instance, a man's mother dies. Instinctively conscience

begins to speak in him. To love, to honor and to cherish one's mother is the duty of every man, but a man is seldom a good son. When his mother dies, a man remembers how he had behaved toward her, and begins to suffer from the gnawings of conscience. But man is a great swine; he very soon forgets, and again lives in the old way.

He who has no conscience cannot be moral. I may know what I should not do, but, through weakness, I cannot refrain from doing it. For instance: I know—I was told by the doctor —that coffee is bad for me. But when I want some coffee I remember only about coffee. It is only when I don't want any coffee that I agree with the doctor and don't drink it. When I am full, I can be moral to a certain extent.

You should forget about morality. Conversations about morality would now be simply empty talk.

Inner morality is your aim. Your aim is to be Christian. But for that you must be able to do—and you cannot. When you are able to do, you will become Christian.

But I repeat, external morality is different everywhere. One should behave like others and, as the saying goes, when in Rome do as the Romans do. This is external morality.

For internal morality a man must be able to do, and for this he must have an I. The first thing that is necessary is to separate inner things from outer, just as I have said about internal and external considering.

For instance, I am sitting here, and although I am used to sitting with my legs crossed under me, I consider the opinion of those present, what they are accustomed to, and I sit as they do, with my legs down.

Now someone gives me a disapproving look. This immediately starts corresponding associations in my feeling, and I am annoyed. I am too weak to refrain from reacting, from considering internally.

Or, for example, although I know that coffee is bad for me I also know that if I don't drink it I shall not be able to talk, I shall feel too tired. I consider my body, and drink the coffee, doing it for my body.

Usually we live like that; what we feel inside we manifest outside. But a boundary line should be established between the inner and the outer, and one should learn to refrain from reacting inwardly to anything, not to consider outer impacts, but externally sometimes to consider more than we do now. For instance, when we have to be polite, we should if necessary learn to be even more polite than we have been till now. It can be said that what has always been inside should now be outside, and what was outside should be inside.

Unfortunately, we always react. For example, if I am angry everything in me is angry, every manifestation. I can learn to be polite when I am angry, but I remain the same inside. But if I use common sense, why should I be angry with someone who gives me a disapproving look? Perhaps he does it out of foolishness. Or perhaps someone turned him against me. He is the slave of someone else's opinion—an automaton, a parrot repeating other people's words. Tomorrow he may change his opinion. If he is weak, I, if I am annoyed, am still weaker, and I may spoil my relationship with others if I am angry with him, making a mountain out of a molehill.

You should understand and establish it as a strict rule that you must not pay attention to other people's opinions, you must be free of the people surrounding you. When you are free inside, you will be free of them.

Outwardly, at times, it may be necessary to pretend to be annoyed. For instance, you may have to pretend to be angry. If you are struck on one cheek, it does not necessarily mean that you must offer the other cheek. Sometimes it is necessary to answer back in such a way that the other will forget his grandmother. But internally one should not consider.

If you are free inwardly it may happen sometimes that if someone strikes you on one cheek, you should offer the other. This depends on a man's type. Sometimes the other will not forget such a lesson in a hundred years.

At times one should retaliate, at other times not. It is necessary to adjust yourself to your circumstances—now you cannot because you are inside out. You must discriminate among your inner associations. Then you can separate, and recognize every thought, but for that it is necessary to ask and to think why. Choice of action is possible only if a man is free inside. An ordinary man cannot choose, he cannot form a critical estimate of the situation; with him, his external is his internal. It is necessary to learn to be unbiased, to sort out and analyze each action as though one were a stranger. Then one can be just. To be just at the very moment of action is a hundred times more valuable than to be just afterwards. A great deal is necessary for this. An unbiased attitude is the basis of inner freedom, the first step toward free will.

Question: Is it necessary to suffer all the time to keep conscience open?

Answer: Suffering can be of very different kinds. Suffering is also a stick with two ends. One leads to the angel, the other to the devil. One must remember the swing of the pendulum, and that after great suffering there is proportionately great reaction. Man is a very complicated machine. By the side of every good road there runs a corresponding bad one. One thing is always side by side with the other. Where there is little good there is also little bad; where there is much good there is also much bad. The same with suffering—it is easy to find oneself on the wrong road. Suffering easily becomes pleasurable. You are hit once, you are hurt; the second time you are less hurt; the fifth time you already wish to be hit. One must be on guard, one must know what is necessary at each moment, because one can stray off the road into a ditch.

Question: What is the relation of conscience to the acquisition of I?

Answer: Conscience helps only in that it saves time. A man who has conscience is calm; a man who is calm has time which he can use for work. However, conscience serves this purpose only in the beginning, later it serves another purpose.

Fears — identification

Sometimes a man is lost in revolving thoughts which return again and again to the same thing, the same unpleasantness, which he anticipates and which not only will not but cannot happen in reality.

These forebodings of future unpleasantnesses, illnesses, losses, awkward situations often get hold of a man to such an extent that they become waking dreams. People cease to see and hear what actually happens, and if someone succeeds in proving to them that their forebodings and fears were unfounded in some particular instance, they even feel a certain disappointment, as though they were thus deprived of a pleasant expectation.

Very often a man leading a cultured life in cultured surroundings does not realize how big a role fears play in his life. He is afraid of everything: afraid of his servants, afraid of the children of his neighbor, the porter in the entrance hall, the man selling newspapers around the corner, the cab-driver, the shop assistant, a friend he sees in the street and tries to pass unobtrusively so as not to be noticed. And in their turn the children, the servants, the hall porter, and so on, are afraid of him.

And this is so in ordinary, normal times but, at such times as we are going through, now, this all-pervading fear becomes clearly visible.

It is no exaggeration to say that a great part of the events of the last year are based on fear and are the results of fear.

Unconscious fear is a very characteristic feature of sleep.

Man is possessed by all that surrounds him because he can never look sufficiently objectively on his relationship to his surroundings.

He can never stand aside and look at himself together with whatever attracts or repels him at the moment. And because of this inability he is identified with everything.

This too is a feature of sleep.

You begin a conversation with someone with the definite aim of getting some information from him. To attain this aim you must never cease to watch yourself, to remember what you want, to stand aside and look at yourself and the man you are talking to. But you cannot do it. Nine times out of ten you will become identified with the conversation and instead of getting the information you want, you will yourself tell him things you had no intention of telling.

People have no idea how much they are carried away by fear. This fear is not easily defined. More often than not it is fear of awkward situations, fear of what another man may think. At times this fear becomes almost a mania.

Man is subject to many influences, which can be divided into two categories. First, those which result from chemical and physical causes, and second, those which are associative in origin and are a result of our conditioning.

Chemico-physical influences are material in nature and result from the mixture of two substances which produce something new. They arise independently of us. They act from without.

For example, someone's emanations may combine with mine —the mixture produces something new. And this is true not only of external emanations; the same thing also happens inside a man.

You perhaps have noticed that you feel at ease or ill at ease when someone is sitting close to you. When there is no accord, we feel ill at ease.

Each man has different kinds of emanations, with their own laws, allowing of various combinations.

Emanations of one center form various combinations with emanations of another center. This kind of combination is chemical. Emanations vary, even depending on whether I had tea or coffee.

Associative influences are quite different. If someone pushes

[254]

me or weeps, the resulting action on me is mechanical. It touches off some memory and this memory or association gives rise in me to other associations, and so on. Owing to this shock my feelings, my thoughts change. Such a process is not chemical but mechanical.

These two kinds of influences come from things that are near to us. But there are also other influences which come from big things, from the earth, from the planets and from the sun, where laws of a different order operate. At the same time there are many influences of these great entities which cannot reach us if we are wholly under the influence of small things.

First, to speak about chemico-physical influences. I said that man has several centers. I spoke about the carriage, the horse and the driver, and also about the shafts, the reins and the ether. Everything has its emanations and its atmosphere. The nature of each atmosphere is different from others because each has a different origin, each has different properties, and a different content. They are similar to one another, but the vibrations of their matter differ.

The carriage, our body, has an atmosphere with its own special properties.

My feelings also produce an atmosphere, the emanations of which may go a long way.

When I think as a result of my associations, the result is emanations of a third kind.

When there is a passenger instead of an empty place in the carriage, emanations are also different, distinct from the emanations of the driver. The passenger is not a country bumpkin; he thinks of philosophy and not about whiskey.

Thus every man may have four kinds of emanations, but not necessarily. Of some emanations he may have more, of others less. People are different in this respect; and one and the same man may also be different at different times. I had coffee but he hadn't—the atmosphere is different. I smoke but she sighs.

There is always interaction, at times bad for me, at other

times good. Every minute I am this or that, and around me it is so or so. And the influences inside me also vary. I can change nothing. I am a slave. These influences I call chemico-physical.

Associative influences, on the other hand, are quite different. Let us take first the associative influences on me of "form." Form influences me. I am accustomed to see a particular form, and when it is absent I am afraid. Form gives the initial shock to my associations. For example, beauty is also form. In reality we cannot see form as it is, we only see an image.

The second of these associative influences is my feelings, my sympathies or antipathies.

Your feelings affect me, my feelings react correspondingly. But sometimes it happens the other way round. It depends on the combinations. Either you influence me or I influence you. This influence may be called "relationship."

The third of these associative influences may be called "persuasion" or "suggestion." For example, one man persuades another with words. One persuades you, you persuade another. Everybody persuades, everybody suggests.

The fourth of these associative influences is the superiority of one man over another. Here there may be no influence of form or feeling. You may know that a given man is more clever, wealthier, can talk about certain things; in a word, possesses something special, some authority. This affects you because it is superior to you, and it happens without any feelings.

So these are eight kinds of influences. Half of them are chemico-physical, the other half associative.

In addition there exist other influences which affect us most seriously. Every moment of our life, every feeling and thought is colored by planetary influences. To these influences also we are slaves.

I shall dwell only briefly on this aspect and shall then return to the main subject. Don't forget what we have been speaking about. Most people are inconsistent and constantly stray from the subject.

The earth and all other planets are in constant motion, each with a different velocity. Sometimes they approach one another, at other times they recede from one another. Their mutual interaction is thus intensified or weakened, or even ceases altogether. Generally speaking, planetary influences on the earth alternate: now one planet acts, now another, now a third, and so on. Some day we shall examine the influence of each planet separately, but at present, in order to give you a general idea, we shall take them in their totality.

Schematically we can picture these influences in the following way. Imagine a big wheel, hanging upright above the earth, with seven or nine enormous colored spotlights fixed round the rim. The wheel revolves, and the light of now one and now another projector is directed toward the earth—thus the earth is always colored by the light of the particular projector which illuminates it at a given moment.

All beings born on earth are colored by the light prevailing at the moment of birth, and keep this color throughout life. Just as no effect can be without cause, so no cause can be without effect. And indeed planets have a tremendous influence both on the life of mankind in general and on the life of every individual man. It is a great mistake of modern science not to recognize this influence. On the other hand this influence is not so great as modern "astrologers" would have us believe.

Man is a product of the interaction of three kinds of matter: positive (atmosphere of the earth), negative (minerals, metals) and a third combination, planetary influences, which comes from outside and meets these two matters. This neutralizing force is the planetary influence which colors each newly born life. This coloring remains for the whole of its existence. If the color was red, then when this life meets with red it feels in correspondence with it.

Certain combinations of colors have a calming effect, others a disturbing effect. Each color has its own peculiar property. There is a law in this; it depends on chemical differences. There are, so to speak, congenial and uncongenial combinations. For instance, red stimulates anger, blue awakens love. Pugnacity corresponds to yellow. Thus if I am apt to lose my temper suddenly, this is due to the influence of the planets.

It does not mean that you or I are actually like that, but we may be. There may be stronger influences. Sometimes another influence acts from within and prevents you from feeling the external influence; you may have such a strong preoccupation that you are, as it were, encased in armor. And this is so not only with planetary influences. Often a distant influence cannot reach you. The more remote the influence, the weaker it is. And even if it were specially sent to you, it might not reach you because your armor would prevent it.

The more developed a man is, the more he is subject to influences. Sometimes, wishing to free ourselves from influences, we get free of one and fall under many others and so become even less free, even more slaves.

We have spoken of nine influences.

Always everything influences us. Every thought, feeling, movement is a result of one or another influence. Everything we do, all our manifestations are what they are because something influences us from without. Sometimes this slavery humiliates us, sometimes not; it depends on what we like. We are also under many influences which we share in common with animals. We may want to get free from one or two, but having got free of them we may acquire another ten. On the other hand we do have some choice, that is, we can keep some and free ourselves of others. It is possible to become free of two kinds of influences.

To free oneself of chemico-physical influences, one has to be passive. I repeat, these are the influences which are due to the emanations of the atmosphere of the body, of feeling, of thought, and in some people also of ether. To be able to resist these influences one has to be passive. Then one can become a little freer of them. The law of attraction operates here. Like attracts like. That is, everything goes toward the place where there is more of the same kind. To him who has much, more is given. From him who has little, even that is taken away.

If I am calm, my emanations are heavy so other emanations come to me and I can absorb them, as much as I have room for. But if I am agitated I have not enough emanations, for they are going out to others.

If emanations come to me, they occupy empty places, for they are necessary where there is a vacuum.

Emanations remain where there is calm, where there is no friction, where there is an empty place. If there is no room, if everything is full, emanations may hit against me but they rebound or pass by. If I am calm, I have an empty place so I can receive them; but if I am full they do not trouble me. So I am ensured in either case.

To become free of influences of the second, that is, the associative kind, requires an artificial struggle. Here the law of repulsion acts. This law consists in the fact that where there is little, more is added, that is, it is the reverse of the first law. With influences of this kind everything proceeds according to the law of repulsion.

So for freeing oneself from influences there are two separate principles for the two different kinds of influences. If you want to be free you must know which principle to apply in every particular case. If you apply repulsion where attraction is needed, you will be lost. Many do the reverse of what is required. It is very easy to discriminate between these two influences; it can be done at once.

In the case of other influences one has to know a great deal. But these two kinds of influences are simple; everyone, if he takes the trouble to look, can see what kind of influence it is. But some people, although they know that emanations exist, don't know the difference between them. Yet, it is easy to distinguish emanations if one observes them closely. It is very interesting to embark upon such a study; every day one obtains greater results, one acquires a taste for discrimination. But it is very difficult to explain it theoretically.

It is impossible to obtain a result immediately, and become free from these influences at once. But study and discrimination are possible for everyone.

Change is a distant goal, requiring much time and labor. But study does not take much time. Still, if you prepare yourselves for the change, it will be less difficult, you won't need to waste time on discrimination.

To study the second or associative kind of influence is easier in practice. For instance, take influence through form. Either you or I influence the other. But form is external: movements, clothes, cleanliness or otherwise—what is generally called the "mask." If you understand, you can easily change it. For example, he likes you in black and, through that, you can influence him. Or she can influence you. But do you wish to change your dress only for him or for many? Some want to do it only for him, others not. Sometimes a compromise is necessary.

Never take anything literally. I say this only as an example.

As regards the second kind of associative influence, what we have called feeling and relationship, we should know that the attitude of others toward us depends on us. In order to live intelligently, it is very important to understand that the responsibility for almost every good or bad feeling lies in you, in your outer and inner attitude. The attitude of other people often reflects your own attitude: you begin and the other person does the same. You love, she loves. You are cross, she is cross. It is a law—you receive what you give.

But sometimes it is different. Sometimes one should love one and not love another. Sometimes if you like her she does not like you, but as soon as you cease to like her she begins to like you. This is due to chemico-physical laws.

Everything is the result of three forces: everywhere there is affirmation and negation, cathode and anode. Man, earth, everything is like a magnet. The difference is only in the quantity of emanations. Everywhere two forces are at work, one attracting, another repelling. As I said, man is also a magnet. The right hand pushes, the left hand pulls, or vice versa. Some things have many emanations, some less, but everything attracts or repels. Always there is push and pull, or pull and push. When you have your push and pull well-balanced with another, then you have love and right adjustment. Therefore results may be very different. If I push and he pulls correspondingly, or if the same thing is done not correspondingly, the result is different. Sometimes both he and I repulse. If there is a certain correspondence, the resulting influence is calming. If not, it is the reverse.

One thing depends on another. For instance, I cannot be calm; I push and he pulls. Or I cannot be calm if I cannot alter the situation. But we can attempt some adjustment. There is a law that after a push there is a pause. We can use this pause if we can prolong it and not rush forward to the next push. If we can be quiet, then we can take advantage of the vibrations which follow a push.

Everyone can stop for there is a law that everything moves only so long as momentum lasts. Then it stops. Either he or I can stop it. Everything happens in this way. A shock to the brain, and vibrations start. Vibrations go on by momentum, similar to rings on the surface of water if a stone is thrown in. If the impact is strong, a long time elapses before the movement subsides. The same happens with vibrations in the brain. If I don't continue to give shocks, they stop, quiet down. One should learn to stop them.

If I act consciously, the interaction will be conscious. If I act unconsciously, everything will be the result of what I am sending out.

I affirm something; then he begins to deny it. I say this is black; he knows it is black but is inclined to argue and begins to assert that it is white. If I deliberately agree with him, he will turn around and affirm what he denied before. He cannot agree because every shock provokes in him the opposite. If he grows tired he may agree externally, but not internally. For example, I see you, I like your face. This new shock, stronger than the conversation, makes me agree externally. Sometimes you already believe but you continue to argue.

It is very interesting to observe other people's conversation, if one is oneself out of it. It is much more interesting than the cinema. Sometimes two people speak of the same thing: one affirms something, another does not understand, but argues, although he is of the same opinion.

Everything is mechanical.

About relationships, it can be formulated like this: our external relationships depend on us. We can change them if we take the necessary measures.

The third kind of influence, suggestion, is very powerful. Every person is under the influence of suggestion; one person suggests to another. Many suggestions occur very easily, especially if we don't know that we are being exposed to suggestion. But even if we do know, suggestions penetrate.

It is very important to understand one law. As a rule, at every moment of our life only one center works in us—either mind or feeling. Our feeling is of one kind when another center is not looking on, when the ability to criticize is absent. By itself a center has no consciousness, no memory; it is a chunk of a particular kind of meat without salt, an organ, a certain combination of substances which merely possesses a special capacity of recording.

Indeed it greatly resembles the coating of a recording tape. If I say something to it, it can later repeat it. It is completely mechanical, organically mechanical. All centers differ slightly as to their substance, but their properties are the same.

Now, if I say to one center that you are beautiful, it believes it. If I tell it that this is red—it also believes. But it does not understand—its understanding is quite subjective. Later, if I

Influences [263]

ask it a question, it repeats in reply what I have said. It will
not change in a hundred, in a thousand years—it will always
remain the same. Our mind has no critical faculty in itself, no
consciousness, nothing. And all the other centers are the same.

What then is our consciousness, our memory, our critical
faculty? It's very simple. It is when one center specially
watches another, when it sees and feels what is going on there
and, seeing it, records it all within itself.

It receives new impressions, and later, if we wish to know
what happened the previous time, if we ask and search in another center, we will be able to find what has taken place in
the first center. It is the same with our critical faculty—one
center watches another. With one center we know that this
thing is red, but another center sees it as blue. One center is
always trying to persuade another. This is what criticism is.

If two centers go on for a long time disagreeing about something, this disagreement hinders us in thinking about it further.

If another center is not watching, the first continues to think
as it did originally. We very seldom watch one center from another, only sometimes, perhaps one minute a day. When we
sleep we never look at one center from another, we do so only
sometimes when we are awake.

In the majority of cases each center lives its own life. It believes everything it hears, without criticism, and records
everything as it has heard it. If it hears something it has heard
before, it simply records. If something it hears is incorrect, for
instance, something was red before and is blue now, it resists,
not because it wants to find out what is right but simply because it does not immediately believe. But it does believe, it
believes everything. If something is different, it only needs
time for perceptions to settle down. If another center is not
watching at the moment, it puts blue over red. And so blue
and red remain together and later, when we read the records,
it begins to answer: "red." But "blue" is just as likely to pop
out.

It is possible for us to ensure a critical perception of new material if we take care that, during perception, another center should stand by and perceive this material from aside. Supposing I now say something new. If you listen to me with one center, there will be nothing new for you in what I am saying; you need to listen differently. Otherwise as there was nothing before, so there will be nothing now. The value will be the same: blue will be red, or vice versa, and again there will be no knowledge. Blue may become yellow.

If you wish to hear new things in a new way, you must listen in a new way. This is necessary not only in the work but also in life. You can become a little more free in life, more secure, if you begin to be interested in all new things and remember them by new methods. This new method can be understood easily. It would no longer be wholly automatic but semi-automatic. This new method consists in the following: when thought is already there, try to feel. When you feel something, try to direct your thoughts on your feeling. Up to now, thought and feeling have been separated.

Begin to watch your mind: feel what you think. Prepare for tomorrow and safeguard yourselves from deceit. Speaking generally, you will never understand what I wish to convey if you merely listen.

Take all you already know, all you have read, all you have seen, all you have been shown—I am certain that you understand nothing of it. Even if you ask yourselves sincerely, do you understand why two and two make four, you will find that you are not sure even of that. You only heard someone else say so, and you repeat what you have heard. And not only in questions of daily life, but also in higher serious matters, you understand nothing. All that you have is not yours.

You have a garbage can and, until now, you have been dumping things into it. There are many precious things in it which you could make use of. There are specialists who collect all kinds of refuse from garbage cans; some make a lot of

money this way. In your garbage cans you have enough material to understand everything. If you understand, you will
know everything. There is no need to gather more into this
garbage can—everything is there. But there is no understanding—the place of understanding is quite empty.

You may have a great deal of money that does not belong to
you, but you would be better off to have far less, even a
hundred dollars that is your own, but nothing you have is
yours.

A large idea should be taken only with large understanding.
For us, small ideas are all we are capable of understanding—if
even these. Generally it is better to have a little thing inside
than something big outside.

Do it very slowly. You can take anything you like and think
about it, but think in a different way than you have thought
before.

Liberation leads to liberation.

These are the first words of truth—not truth in quotation marks but truth in the real meaning of the word; truth which is not merely theoretical, not simply a word, but truth that can be realized in practice. The meaning behind these words may be explained as follows:

By liberation is meant the liberation which is the aim of all schools, all religions, at all times.

This liberation can indeed be very great. All men desire it and strive after it. But it cannot be attained without the first liberation, a lesser liberation. The great liberation is liberation from influences outside us. The lesser liberation is liberation from influences within us.

At first, for beginners, this lesser liberation appears to be very great, for a beginner depends very little on external influences. Only a man who has already become free of inner influences falls under external influences.

Inner influences prevent a man from falling under external influences. Maybe it is for the best. Inner influences and inner slavery come from many varied sources and many independent factors—independent in that sometimes it is one thing and sometimes another, for we have many enemies.

There are so many of these enemies that life would not be long enough to struggle with each of them and free ourselves from each one separately. So we must find a method, a line of work, which will enable us simultaneously to destroy the greatest possible number of enemies within us from which these influences come.

I said that we have many independent enemies, but the chief and most active are vanity and self-love. One teaching even calls them representatives and messengers of the devil himself.

For some reason they are also called Mrs. Vanity and Mr. Self-Love.

As I have said, there are many enemies. I have mentioned only these two as the most fundamental. At the moment it is hard to enumerate them all. It would be difficult to work on each of them directly and specifically, and it would take too much time since there are so many. So we have to deal with them indirectly in order to free ourselves from several at once.

These representatives of the devil stand unceasingly at the threshold which separates us from the outside, and prevent not only good but also bad external influences from entering. Thus they have a good side as well as a bad side.

For a man who wishes to discriminate among the influences he receives, it is an advantage to have these watchmen. But if a man wishes all influences to enter, no matter what they may be—for it is impossible to select only the good ones—he must liberate himself as much as possible, and finally altogether, from these watchmen, whom some consider undesirable.

For this there are many methods, and a great number of means. Personally I would advise you to try freeing yourselves and to do so without unnecessary theorizing, by simple reasoning, active reasoning, with yourselves.

Through active reasoning this is possible, but if anyone does not succeed, if he fails to do so by this method, there are no other means for what is to follow.

Take, for instance, self-love, which occupies almost half of our time and our life. If someone, or something, has wounded our self-love from outside, then, not only at that moment but for a long time afterwards, its momentum closes all the doors, and therefore shuts out life.

When I am connected with outside, I live. If I live only inside myself, it is not life; but everybody lives thus. When I examine myself, I connect myself with the outside.

For instance, now I sit here. M. is here and also K. We live together. M. called me a fool—I am offended. K. gave me a scornful look—I am offended. I consider, I am hurt and shall not calm down and come to myself for a long time.

All people are so affected, all have similar experiences the whole time. One experience subsides, but no sooner has it subsided than another of the same nature starts. Our machine is so arranged that there are no separate places where different things can be experienced simultaneously.

We have only one place for our psychic experiences. And so if this place is occupied with such experiences as these, there can be no question of our having the experiences we desire. And if certain attainments or liberations are supposed to bring us to certain experiences, they will not do so if things remain as they are.

M. called me a fool. Why should I be offended? Such things do not hurt me, so I don't take offense—not because I have no self-love; maybe I have more self-love than anyone here. Maybe it is this very self-love that does not let me be offended.

I think, I reason in a way exactly the reverse of the usual way. He called me a fool. Must he necessarily be wise? He himself may be a fool or a lunatic. One cannot demand wisdom from a child. I cannot expect wisdom from him. His reasoning was foolish. Either someone has said something to him about me, or he has formed his own foolish opinion that I am a fool—so much the worse for him. I know that I am not a fool, so it does not offend me. If a fool has called me a fool, I am not affected inside.

But if in a given instance I was a fool and am called a fool, I am not hurt, because my task is not to be a fool; I assume this to be everyone's aim. So he reminds me, helps me to realize that I am a fool and acted foolishly. I shall think about it and perhaps not act foolishly next time.

So, in either case I am not hurt.

K. gave me a scornful look. It does not offend me. On the contrary, I feel sorry for him because of the dirty look he gave me. For a dirty look must have a reason behind it. Can he have such a reason?

I know myself. I can judge from my knowledge of myself. He gave me a dirty look. Possibly someone had told him something that made him form a bad opinion of me. I am sorry for him because he is so much a slave that he looks at me through other people's eyes. This proves that he is not. He is a slave and so he cannot hurt me.

I say all this as an example of reasoning.

Actually, the secret and the cause of all such things lies in the fact that we do not possess ourselves nor do we possess genuine self-love. Self-love is a great thing. If we consider self-love, as we generally understand it, as reprehensible, then it follows that true self-love—which, unfortunately, we do not possess—is desirable and necessary.

Self-love is a sign of a high opinion of oneself. If a man has this self-love it proves what he is.

As we have said earlier, self-love is a representative of the devil; it is our chief enemy, the main brake to our aspirations and our achievements. Self-love is the principal weapon of the representative of hell.

But self-love is an attribute of the soul. By self-love one can discern the spirit. Self-love indicates and proves that a given man is a particle of heaven. Self-love is I—I is God. Therefore it is desirable to have self-love.

Self-love is hell, and self-love is heaven. These two, bearing the same name, are outwardly alike, but totally different and opposite to one another in essence. But if we look superficially, we can go on looking throughout our whole life without ever distinguishing the one from the other.

There exists a saying: "He who has self-love is halfway to freedom." Yet, among those sitting here, everyone is full to over-flowing with self-love. And in spite of the fact that we are full to the brim with self-love, we have not yet attained one tiny bit of freedom. Our aim must be to have self-love. If we have self-love, by this very fact we shall become free of many enemies in us. We can even become free of these principal ones—Mr. Self-Love and Mrs. Vanity.

How to distinguish between one kind of self-love and an-other? We have said that on the surface it is very difficult. This is so even when we look at others; when we look at our-selves it is still more difficult.

Thank God we, who are sitting here, are safe from confusing the one with the other. We are lucky! Genuine self-love is to-tally absent, so there is nothing to confuse.

In the beginning of the lecture I used the words "active reasoning."

Active reasoning is learned by practice; it should be prac-ticed long and in many varied ways.

VI

The aphorisms

*inscribed in a special script above the
walls of the Study House at the Prieuré*

1. Like what "it" does not like.

2. The highest that a man can attain is to be able to do.

3. The worse the conditions of life the more productive the
   work, always provided you remember the work.

4. Remember yourself always and everywhere.

5. Remember you come here having already understood the
   necessity of struggling with yourself—only with yourself.
   Therefore thank everyone who gives you the opportunity.

6. Here we can only direct and create conditions, but not
   help.

7. Know that this house can be useful only to those who have
   recognized their nothingness and who believe in the possibility of changing.

8. If you already know it is bad and do it, you commit a sin
   difficult to redress.

9. The chief means of happiness in this life is the ability to consider externally always, internally never.

10. Do not love art with your feelings.

11. A true sign of a good man is if he loves his father and mother.

12. Judge others by yourself and you will rarely be mistaken.

13. Only help him who is not an idler.

14. Respect every religion.

15. I love him who loves work.

16. We can only strive to be able to be Christians.

17. Don't judge a man by the tales of others.

18. Consider what people think of you—not what they say.

19. Take the understanding of the East and the knowledge of the West—and then seek.

20. Only he who can take care of what belongs to others may have his own.

21. Only conscious suffering has any sense.

22. It is better to be temporarily an egoist than never to be just.

23. Practice love first on animals, they are more sensitive.

24. By teaching others you will learn yourself.

25. Remember that here work is not for work's sake but is only a means.

26. Only he can be just who is able to put himself in the position of others.

27. If you have not by nature a critical mind your staying here is useless.

28. He who has freed himself of the disease of "tomorrow" has a chance to attain what he came here for.

29. Blessed is he who has a soul, blessed is he who has none, but woe and grief to him who has it in embryo.

30. Rest comes not from the quantity but from the quality of sleep.

31. Sleep little without regret.

32. The energy spent on active inner work is then and there transformed into a fresh supply, but that spent on passive work is lost for ever.

33. One of the best means for arousing the wish to work on yourself is to realize that you may die at any moment. But first you must learn how to keep it in mind.

34. Conscious love evokes the same in response. Emotional love evokes the opposite. Physical love depends on type and polarity.

35. Conscious faith is freedom. Emotional faith is slavery. Mechanical faith is foolishness.

36. Hope, when bold, is strength. Hope, with doubt, is coward-
ice. Hope, with fear, is weakness.

37. Man is given a definite number of experiences—econo-
mizing them, he prolongs his life.

38. Here there are neither Russians nor English, Jews nor
Christians, but only those who pursue one aim—
to be able to be.